The Salmon Run

One Man's Journey to Personal Freedom

By

Eduardo F Calcines

A work by Eduardo F Calcines.

To my grandson Luke,

and in memory of my mother, Dionisia

To Billy Graham—I am forever grateful.

"Man has two great spiritual needs. One is for forgiveness.

The other is for goodness." - *Billy Graham*

'Perhaps if you are fortunate enough to have loved a place in time enough to die for, then wherever you go for the rest of your life, it stays with you. Its memories remain engraved upon the walls of your heart, as you hope to someday return. It's like the Salmon, whose lifelong purpose is to return to its natal stream to spawn—so was Manolo's passion for freedom! In some mysterious way, that's how the old man saw it.

If the readers of this book prefer, this story can be regarded as fiction, but there is always the chance that such a story may have occurred in fact.

Contents

Introduction

A life scarred by the pain of losing his mother and his young wife, had deeply afflicted the old seaman, Manolo. In some mysterious way he associated the return to his beloved birthplace, to the salmon's run back to their natal stream.

The squinting spark in Manolo's eyes when he spoke of vengeance against the one man he blamed for the death of his loved ones was eminent among those who knew him. Nothing else mattered to the old man—killing Fidel Castro had been his purpose ever since he had escaped the island prison twenty years prior. In young Pablo, Manolo had finally found an accomplice who would join him on his lifelong mission and whose hatred for the Cuban dictator ran as deep as his own. Struggling with an unquenchable craving for payback, Pablo also dreamed of the day when he could even the score with the dictator on behalf of his family. Then, in the midst of an uprising in Habana, it

happened. Pablo was granted the opportunity to realize his

dream. *The mission,* silence the bastards voice permanently.

Chapter One

The Voice

Pablo once lived in a world filled with love, but that world changed when he was three. Although too young to remember much, he remembered spending much of his time alone and feeling sad. As he grew up, he realized why his world had changed for the worst—it was the voice on the radio, then he saw the face of the man and despised him.

Having been raised to be a person of faith, Pablo knew killing was not pleasing to God. His Abuelo *or* Grandfather Julian had reminded him of this since he was a child. But no matter what anyone said, Pablo's hatred towards the man with the voice on the radio became obsessive. He was the one person Pablo blamed for the breakup of his large and happy family, as well as his turbulent childhood. The bearded young Cuban leader, to whom the voice belonged, believed in creating a new man who was to care more for the state, God, family or friends. *Divide and conquer was the method to his madness,* Pablo's papa Felo once said.

Being only a child, Pablo didn't know much about life or politics and even less about what his Papa meant when he said *divide and conquer.* What he did know was what his own eyes saw, as the once loving family turned on one another because of political differences.

Pablo was almost 4 when the Communist took over power of Cuba in 1959. In his childlike memory, that is when the world changed for his Abuelo, Julian and him. Pablo remembers hearing the voice of a man on the radio, who spoke of great things to come while damming the imperialist Yankees in America. The man also spoke of shaming those who didn't join the Cuban Communist party.

Then one day while watching television with his Abuelo, Pablo saw the man to whom the voice belonged. He was a tall bearded man dressed in olive green military uniform; he wore a green cap with a golden star pinned on the front. The man with the voice stood high upon a public podium, surrounded by other bearded men in uniform with guns strapped to their side.

On that day, Pablo also saw countless spectators standing in awe of the man with the long beard and the loud voice. In the innocence of his childhood, Pablo thought the man on the podium had supernatural powers. Every time he finished a statement and pointed his index finger up in the air, the spectators roared with applause while passionately chanting "Fidel, Fidel…"

Then he noticed his Abuelo's facial reaction from the corner of his eyes, it was obvious he thought differently than the masses. To most people, the young bearded leader was a savior and a hero—Abuelo, Julian knew better. Although he did not support the previous Cuban dictator Fulgencio Batista, Julian was leery of the young Castro. At the age of eighty two, he had lived a long life and had seen many things, especially the falsehood of passed politicians who promised the world and delivered deceit. To Julian, Castro was like the rest—yet worse.

"He is a narcissist in the likes of men like Hitler," Abuelo, Julian would often say in family gatherings. "Proof of it," he'd continue, "Fidel's love of Adolf Hitler's book, *Mein Kampf, or* My Struggle. He read it daily while serving prison time for attempting to over-through the Batista government in 1953.

"I know what I'm saying," Julian would say. "Trust me, he is worse!"

Pablo didn't really understand who the bearded revolutionaries were, but something about them was making his Abuelo, Julian upset. In the closeness of their relationship, Pablo felt his Abuelo's concern, making him upset. All Pablo wanted was to see him happy, so they could play catch in the backyard and chase butterflies once again.

No one doubted Julian's knowledge of world politics or his spiritual discernment; he was a God-fearing man who had lived a spotless life in accordance to his faith. In Pablo's eyes, Abuelo Julian was just short of sainthood—when he spoke, everyone listened.

As time passed, Pablo noticed the adults in his family didn't laugh much anymore, especially Julian. Although too young to remember much, Pablo remembered images on television of a street parade in Havana, as the revolution rebels made their way into the capital city. He remembered people dancing in the streets next to slow rolling trucks and floats packed with bearded men dressed in green uniforms, festively waving their guns in the air. Pablo also remembered the large crowds cheering on the revolutionaries while chanting, *"Viva la Revolución," or* long live the Revolution." He also remembered solemn moments while he sat next to his Abuelo and not a word was uttered for extended periods of time. Silence that would periodically be

15

interrupted by the sandy sound of Julian's aged hands running through his silky white hair, while he shook his head in disbelief.

"I don't like the look of those men boy," he'd say to Pablo. "Our lives are about to change for the worse."

Pablo was too naive to know what his Abuelo meant, but going by the sad look on his face, Pablo knew it wasn't good. Julian was king among men for Pablo and seeing him upset was overwhelmingly upsetting to Pablo. To see the hero of his youth be consumed with sadness gave birth to Pablo's blinding hatred of Castro.

Julian had labored all of his life in the sugar cane industry, while helping raise eleven children with his loving wife, Abuela, *or* Grandmother Ana. He had lived through many trials in his long life, yet he feared Castro's revolution might be the worst one of all!

As time passed, Pablo consistently noticed the sorrow in Julian's eyes every time he heard Fidel's voice on the radio. As time passed Pablo's anger for the bearded man continued to grow. He was the colorful leader of the new revolution and the one person responsible for making his Abuelo sad. To make things worse, every time the man gave a speech on the radio, his supporters took to the streets chanting his name in wild celebrations of government organized marches, while Julian murmured something about the end of freedom in Cuba.

When, at one time he and Pablo could listen to baseball games on the radio for hours, Abuelo Julian didn't seem to care about the national pastime anymore. Like dying a slow painful death, he spoke less with each passing day. No matter how hard Pablo tried to make him happy, his smiles became rare. Although Pablo tried desperately to ignore his sadness, he couldn't sleep at night worrying about his aging king. The only thing that mattered to the new regime was the revolution, not God, not family, not friends—but the revolution. Like a strangle hold that squeezes the life out of a man, the government took greater control of the peoples freedom through intimidation in the form of incarceration or firing squads for those who opposed the new regime, leaving them little alternative, but to live a submissive existence.

Realizing the manipulating control of the newly established government, Pablo's parents decided to apply for a visa to leave the country in pursue of freedom in America. After many years of psychological torture and abuse, Pablo's immediate family eventually escaped to America in 1969, shortly after his fourteenth birthday. Troubled by having to leave his Abuelos behind, Pablo held on to the hope of someday seeing them again in a free Cuba.

Chapter Two

America

Libertad, *or* Freedom, a man screamed with passion from the rear of the plane—his voice filled with emotion. After five tormenting years waiting to leave the island prison of Cuba, Pablo, his sister and parents had finally landed in America!

Folks laughed and cried at the same time inside the plane. They embraced each other and applauded in celebration. Pablo and his immediate family were finally free and nothing could change that. As the plane made its way to the airside at snail pace, Pablo looked at his Mama, Conchita, then his Papa and then sister, while their eyes connected in silent celebration; they then shared a peaceful smile. For a long time Pablo had wondered what being free would feel like, at that moment he knew. Then he thought of his childhood friend Rolando who always spoke of being free in America but he couldn't leave Cuba because his father had joined the Communist Party.

Somberly and with mixed emotions, Pablo looked out of the plane's window and saw the world moving faster than he ever had before. Service trucks smothered the air craft while modern cars rolled on by in the busy distant streets of Miami. Then he saw the flag he had gotten in trouble for drawing while daydreaming in a Mrs. Santana's classroom back home. It was the imposing American flag gently reaching out to greet him while dancing in the wind. *Welcome boy it said to him, "you're are finally free"*

For a moment and in his thoughts of joy, Pablo danced with the impressive red, white and blue in all its glory, he then thought of what it meant for him and his family. No more fear of abuse and humiliation from the Communist were his thoughts. No more food rations, long lines or sleepless nights hearing his Mama cry.

America! Libertad! Many were his thoughts at that moment. At last, they were free!

Once the Pan Am jet had come to a full stop, Pablo noticed his Papa, Felo relax for the first time since they had left Cuba. He also noticed him slapping the side of his leg with his right hand hoping no one would notice. Thinking it was a new twitch, Pablo became concerned.

"Papa, are you twitching again?" Pablo asked concerned.

"Shhh" I am trying to wake up my hand son!"

"Papa," Pablo persisted. "What is wrong with your hand?"

"It's asleep son! I guess I have been holding on to the arm rest too tightly"

"Yeah Papa! Like forty five minutes too tight!"

It took every bit of personal restraint to keep Pablo from bursting out in laughter. He then looked at his Mama and her eyes were as large as goose eggs. The smirk on her

21

face said a thousand words, although not one escaped her hard-pressed lips. Pablo could tell by her expression, she wanted to explode into laughter, but chose not to do so for fear of embarrassing Felo.

Felo had been a twitchy mess throughout the ordeal of leaving Cuba, and even in freedom; it was obvious to Pablo and his Mama, there was no rational hope for his nerves.

Shortly after the plane engines shut off, everyone on board slowly walked into the Miami International airport, where a large welcoming committee of exiled Cubans awaited them with cheers of joy, enhancing the magical experience of the newly found freedom! Shortly after, all the newly arrived passengers were led towards a long line of yellow buses that waited on the service road. Although Pablo was insecure of the unknown, he kept his trusting eyes on the mighty flag, which danced high upon the main airport building. Deep in his heart, Pablo knew it was celebrating their arrival and it knew him by name. The mighty flag also knew of the sorrow and pain of leaving loved ones behind. Many were his thoughts as he walked upon the new land he would now call his own.

"Vamos Para La Casa de la Libertad *or* We are going to the House of Freedom, known earlier as the Miami Freedom Tower," said the man in front of the line, as the group walked toward the buses that awaited the group.

"Que es eso *or* what is that?" Felo asked.

"It is the Cuban Ellis Island," the well dressed man responded.

"Please explain Sir," Felo requested with great interest.

"The Freedom Tower was originally built in 1925, when it housed the offices of the Miami News & Metropolis," the man explained.

"Originally, the tower contained a beacon light to shine over the Miami Bay which symbolically served as a lighthouse, announcing the enlightenment brought by the Miami News & Metropolis to the rest of the world. Unfortunately, the newspaper went out of business 30 years later. The United States federal government now uses the building to provide services to immigrants." The gentleman said.

"How do you know so much about it?" Felo asked with yet greater interest.

The man grinned as if he knew much more. "I just know" he said, then continued.

"That's where the processing of Cuban refugees like us takes place. They provide services such as basic medical and dental checkups, food, clothing and personal research on records of sponsor relatives and churches in the U.S.

"How do you know Sir?" the Papa persisted.

"I was a history professor at the University of Habana before Castro came to power, then after his take over; I was dismissed from my position at the University because I refused to sign on with the medical ideology of the Communist Party. Unable to find work anywhere, I bought a shoe shine box from a neighborhood kid and I went to work on the streets." Papa paused for a moment as to reflect on the gentleman's words, I think the reality that he and his family weren't the only ones being forced out of our country hit him like a brick. The man then continued.

"This is a historic time for all of us." he said while looking at Pablo directly in the eyes.

"What do you mean Sir?" Pablo curiously asked.

The Gentleman stopped for a moment and placed his right on top of Pablo's head, holding it as to make sure Pablo looked at him in the eyes.

"Today we have regained our dignity son—we are free and respected human beings again! Make sure you never forget this day boy, maybe it will be your generation that brings freedom to Cuba someday." He then grinned and walked away.

The gentleman's words dug deep into Pablo's conscience, his Papa Felo twitched once more and shook his head in affirmation of what the gentleman had said. Pablo never saw the man again, but his words remained engraved in his mind.

Comforted by the gentleman's expressions, Felo squeezed Pablo's hand, lifted his head up high and walked ahead with a greater purpose than had throughout their journey to freedom. It was at that moment when he realized that God must have a greater purpose for their lives.

The following hours passed by like a hazy dream. Once on the bus, Pablo's eyes fluttered with wonder at what he saw. It was New Years Eve and the streets of Downtown Miami remained dressed in all the splendor of Christmas. As the caravan of buses traveled west on their way to the House of Freedom, Pablo's eyes remained glued to the world outside. Miami glowed with brilliant decorative colors that flooded his eyes in a spectacle of hope. Pablo had never seen such luxury in his life before. Like a dream, he feared the moment would soon end like many other of his childhood dreams had ended, leaving him the pain of a disillusioned heart.

Upon arrival at the House of Freedom, where the family would be legally processed before heading to their new home in Milwaukee, Wisconsin, where their sponsor family lived, Pablo and his family were escorted to a processing area where American immigration officials welcomed them with kindness and respect.

"Estan contentos?" *or* Are you happy?" One official asked looking at Conchita who covered her mouth filled with emotion.

"Si, muy contentos!" "Yes, very happy!" Conchita joyfully responded.

"America es muy buena, gracias!" *or* America is very good, thank you!"

Shortly after being legally processed, the family was escorted down a long hallway by a lady with a perpetual smile on her face. This must really be a good country if people are so happy all the time, Pablo reflected. None of the officials in Cuba ever smiled, were his thoughts.

After the short walk, they realized the lady had taken them to the cafeteria. Upon arrival, the four of them froze in place when they saw many of the folks who had traveled with them on the plane from Cuba seating on the long tables devouring the food on their plates as if they were cave people. The well mannered lady then led Pablo's family to the buffet line and extended her arm as if to say; there you are—enjoy!

Pablo and his family stood with mouths open, unable to move from the shock of seeing such a large variety of food in one place. Felo smiled and twitched his shoulder a couple of times from happy nerves, but he stopped after he felt

Conchita's elbow on his side, reminding him of proper etiquette in the likes of civilized Americans.

"Look, the servers are motioning for us to go forward," Pablo said excitedly.

"Escojan lo que deceen, *or* choose whatever you want," one of them said nicely.

Going by the look on his face, he must have been a Cuban who had arrived earlier and understood of about the excitement the newly arrived families felt seeing so much food.

"Esto es America, esta es la buena vida que yo esperaba ver," *or* "This is America, this is the good life I had been waiting to see!" Felo said with victorious excitement.

After the shock of the moment, the four of them proceeded to devour everything they put on their plates and then some. They ate hamburgers, hot dogs, French fries, rice and beans and everything they could get our hands on—if it wasn't moving, they stuck a fork in it!

Against Conchitas wishes, Felo made various trips to the buffet line. As if she was still in Cuba, her concern was there wouldn't be enough food for others who followed, and even though Felo wasn't a selfish man, when it came to food, he didn't take a back seat to anyone.

"Felo please, you must be respectful! These nice folks are going to think we just crawled out of a cave."

Felo smiled gently at his dear wife, leaned over close to her face, kissed her and then whispered, "Concha, we were living like animals in a cave back home—this is the USA and just in case you hadn't noticed, we are now free!"

Felo twitched once and proceeded to walk toward the buffet with a cheerful bounce in his steps, looking back at the grinning love of his life, who shook her head in disbelieve. By the time dinner was over and the four had made it back to the room, Felo was ready to explode. Needless to say, he took over the bathroom for the next hour. This was one hour that Conchita laid an unmerciful verbal scolding on him, for having eaten so much. Pablo and Esther chuckled at the agonizing sounds that came from the bathroom while they waited their turn.

When Felo finally made it out, he was pale and exhausted from the laboring experience. The three held their breath for a moment, and then busted out laughing at the look on his face. Felo smiled briefly and then collapsed on the bed holding his stomach and head, begging Conchita for alcohol.

Shortly after his Papa's harrowing experience, the family was called to the processing center on the first floor of the building. Upon arrival, the officials proceeded to inform them that the flight to Milwaukee had been set for 8:00 P.M that evening. The parents had requested a same day flight to Milwaukee, with the hope of arriving there in enough time to celebrate New Year's Eve festivities with the family.

Following the meeting, the family was escorted to a large room filled with racks of clothing and shoes.

"What a generous country this is!" Felo expressed looking around the room in wonder.

Each family member picked a wardrobe and proceeded to change into immediately. They hadn't seen new clothes in years. The next thing Pablo remembers, they were on board a large jet on their way to Milwaukee, where a new life in freedom awaited them.

It had been a long time since they had seen the family in America, especially his cousin Arturito, who years earlier had originated the family's exodus to the US from Cuba. So much had transpired in the years of separation; Pablo couldn't help but wonder how the family reunion would be. Were they the same people they had known before, or had time in the land of plenty changed them? Pablo didn't know what to think, all he knew was that for years he had daydreamed about America and his dream had finally come true.

The flight to Milwaukee went smoothly. Pablo ate and slept, then woke-up long enough to eat and then sleep again. After a while of peaceful rest, he was awakened by the pilot's voice on the overhead speaker. Although Pablo didn't understand what he was saying, he heard something about Milwaukee, and so he figured the plane was preparing to land.

Suddenly, a smile of anticipation dressed Pablo's drowsy face. This time he knew what waited on the other side of the trip—a loving family!

Having flown once before made Pablo feel like an expert in aeronautical engineering in he's own eyes, so as soon as he heard the plane engines slow down, Pablo told his Papa they were landing.

"Que tu sabes niño, *or* what do you know boy?"

"Papa, trust me, we are landing soon," Pablo confirmed with a smirk in his eyes.

That's all Felo needed to hear to once again set him off on one his twitching episodes. He immediately stiffened his neck, fixed his eyes on the front of the plane, grabbed a hold of the seats arm rest and held on so tightly his knuckles turned white.

"Felo, por favor, *or* please!" Mama Conchita whispered holding back the laughter.

"Concha, please relax! I am just doing what I am supposed to do!"

"What are you supposed to do, rip the plane's armrest off?" Conchita asked sarcastically, she then smiled and shook her head knowing that Felo was a hopeless case when it came to flying. He would have rather walked on glass, than to fly in a plane. The only thing that convinced him to remain still was the limited choices he had. Stay in Cuba and live miserably or fly to freedom in America. The choice was clear to him! He just had to endure the agonizing experience of flying a little longer.

"Look Papa the windows of the plane are fogging up! That means we are losing altitude fast." Pablo joyously exclaimed.

"What did you say boy? Loosing what?" Felo asked nervously, his head glued to the head rest of the seat from the minute Pablo told him the plane was losing altitude.

"Never mind Papa, losing altitude just means we are landing soon."

"Landing when? He persisted.

"Oh, forget about it, just hold on Papa." Pablo affirmed, while Felos eyes widened.

"Hold on to what boy?"

"To the seat Papa"

"But I am!" He responded with anxious concern in his voice.

"Felo please, if the plane crashes, it crashes. That just means we will go to be with the Lord sooner." Conchita said with great conviction.

"Okay, okay! But I don't want to go to be with Him yet, I want to know what it feels like to eat ham and cheese, and watch color TV before I go—OK?" Felo responded with wide-eyed.

"Okay Felo. Just sit still and everything will be okay." Conchita said in a calm voice.

Felo complied and held on while closing his eyes, as the wheels of the large-bird hit the ground and landed without incident.

"Look Papa, everything is white, snow is everywhere. It looks like we landed on the moon." Pablo said excited while looking out through the foggy airplane window.

"The moon…what do you mean the moon boy?"

"Never mind Papa, its only snow, we have landed in Milwaukee."

Suddenly Felo loosened the grip on the arm rest. His neck relaxed enough to allow him to turn his head and look outside.

"Wow, that is really snow isn't it?" He said enthusiastically.

It took a minute for them to allow the great spectacle of a winter-whiteout to sink in. Never before had they seen snow and from what they could tell, it really looked like the moon!

Looking at the airport building in the distance as the plane approached the airside; all Pablo could see were vehicle headlights moving from one parked plane to another. The only thing revealing normal human existence was the lights inside the snow covered building which glowed like a lighthouse in the gloominess of a cold winter night. The only thing Pablo could compare it to, was photos he had once seen of an Eskimo igloo in the North Pole.

Although concerned about how he was going to breath in cold weather, the thought of being free in America was superior to the risk of having his lungs freeze in below zero weather.

As the plane came to a complete stop, Pablo heard his Papa exhale the breath he'd been holding for five minutes. Then the thought of something being wrong occurred to him. No one on the plane was celebrating the family's arrival like the trip from Cuba to Miami. As he looked around, everyone was calm and composed. It was then when he realized there were no Cubans in the plane other than him and his family. Suddenly Pablo became aware of the difference between the American and Cuban culture. Americans were very polite and well mannered, not emotional and rambunctious like Cubans.

The family was so happy to have finally landed on their new home, they wanted to hug and kiss everybody around them, yet folks just went about their business, quietly gathering their belongings and lining up to exit the plane in orderly fashion. Looking at his Papa, Pablo thought he would burst from unexpressed joy. He wanted to tell everyone around him of how happy he was to be in America and of his struggles back home in the Communist concentration work camps. But perhaps he figured they wouldn't understand him anyway. Therefore he restrained his emotions, ran his hands through his curly gray hair, fixed the blue scarf he was wearing around his neck, and proceeded to act like the rest of the Americans on the plane.

"I am an American now boy don't you know!" His smirking-happy eyes screamed. Pablo smiled back at him as to let him know he understood.

The short walk out of the airplane and through the airside, leading to the lobby where their family anxiously awaited their arrival, seemed like an eternity. Every step Pablo took towards his new world appeared surreal. He had always wondered what it would feel like to be free. With unavoidable thoughts of those left behind in Glorytown, he continued walking within the wonders of his new world. Pablo could only hope that someday those left behind in Cuba, would have the opportunity to walk in his footsteps, and experience how it felt to be free.

He then saw the airport stores and their display racks full of toys, candy, gum and comic books. It was all too surreal to fully comprehend. So like a zombie he walked with his mouth open, as the emotion of seeing such luxury and abundance got the best of him. Everything slowed down to snail's pace while his eyes wondered in the gleaming lights that surrounded him. Pablo lifted his head towards the lights hoping to keep the tears from flowing, but it was of no use. Then a door at the end of a hall opened automatically and like an act of magical wonder, there they were. At exactly one hour and twenty seven minutes into the year of 1970, Pablo and his family were reunited with their American side of the family after many years of separation.

To be reunited with the Olazabal and the Garcia families in America was a dream come true. Still, the emotional adjustment for Pablo and his family wasn't easy. His Mama Conchita cried nightly, thinking of her parents left behind, knowing that she may never see them again. So much had taken place in so little time—like a foggy dream filled with contradicting emotions.

Life had changed completely for Pablo and his family, suddenly they had to hit the ground running in America—work, school, learning English, drivers license, grocery stores filled with everything a person could want. Decency, kindness and respect, why couldn't Cuba be that way, Pablo wondered from time to time. Impossible, that's not the Communist way, he also thought. Looking at his parents, he thought of their courage, to put their life on hold to save the next generation from the claws of Communism. The government tried to break them down, yet they persevered through five years of emotional abuse, making their day to day lives miserable, while they waited for a visa to leave the country. Worms they were once called—respected Americans they became!

Chapter Three

A Man Called Billy

After five wonder filled years in Milwaukee, Pablo's parents decided to relocate to Tampa, Florida in August of 1974. The cold winters of the Midwest had become too hard on them, especially his father Felo. Saddened by the separation from family and friends once again, Pablo struggled with adjusting to a new life in Tampa. In his eyes, he had acculturated himself to the American way of life in Milwaukee and he was happy with that.

The Latin-based neighborhood of West Tampa where the family first settled, was much like Cuba. The Hispanic culture in Tampa had a long history, dating back to the Spanish American war. The Cuban, Spanish and Italian cultures had finely blended together into the communities of Ybor City and West Tampa. To some degree, this cultural history appealed to Pablo, yet, he soon realized that he had lost a lot of the Cuban in him while in the Midwest. Without realizing it, Pablo had misplaced the Latin lover swagger he once had in the old neighborhood of Glorytown. Americans up north didn't bounce like pimps when they walked, neither did they chew gum with their mouth open, or cut gas indiscriminately. Worst yet, Pablo had never seen so much gold on one person before. Although dumfounded by the culture of his new home, Pablo found Tampa's Latin flavor to be strangely appealing.

The more time passed, the more he reconnected with his deep rooted fervor to see Cuba free once again. His desire to be reunited with his Abuelo's in a free Cuba had never died. Unfortunately and to his great disappointment, they passed away within months of each other in 1975. Their death had blindsided the family, especially his mother, whose greatest hope in life was to see her parent's alive once more. In the blink of an eye, her two angels had fled to heaven without much notice. In a state of disillusionment,

Pablo's mother Conchita, went into a deep depression as the result of their deaths. In her eyes, there had always been hope that Castro would fall from power and she would be able to return to a free Cuba and be together with their family again. In a few short years, life had changed dramatically for Pablo and his family. Throughout his childhood and into his teen years, Pablo's identity had been shaken so many times; he struggled with the meaning of his own existence. The one invariable was his hatred for Castro's regime, and the ever-present desire to terminate the leader's existence.

Just as the pain of his grandparent's death was subsiding, in 1978 his father Felo was stricken with an unknown illness. He had been struggling with stomach discomfort for a while, after two weeks of unsuccessful diagnostic testing, the doctors decided to do exploratory surgery on him. Shortly after the doors to the operating room had closed, they swung open again and out came the surgeon with a somber look upon his face. Felo had been stricken with a rare form of cancer which had metastasized all throughout his major organs. Once again Conchita had been blindsided by the rigors of life, as the surgeon informed her of the prognosis.

"I'm so sorry Señora, *or* Ma'am. Your husband's cancer has a spread rapidly— he has approximately two hours to live."

Overcoming the Doctors initial life expectancy, Felo fought hard to beat the horrible illness. Unfortunately, three months later, Felo lost his battle with cancer; he passed in April of the same year, at the age of 49. Although young, Felo died in peace knowing his family loved him and unlike many of his friends and family members who remained in Cuba unable to escape the island prison, Felo had conquered his goal of getting his family out of Communist Cuba and on to a life of freedom in the United States of America.

Pablo had endured much hardship in his tormenting childhood, yet nothing compared to the despair he felt with his father's death. Fortunately he'd met a lovely girl who had captured his heart a couple of years earlier. Pablo had many relationships in his young life, but he knew this one was different. Meky was refreshingly beautiful and from a good family which had also immigrated to the US from Cuba in 1978. Yet, perhaps most impacting thing Pablo noticed was the fact that she had been raised with strong Christian values.

Unlike many of the girls in the past who came and went, Pablo knew Meky truly cared for him. When other girls would have walked away during the most difficult times, this one stuck with him through it all. Realizing she was special, Pablo committed himself to her and they married later that same year. The way he figured it, Meky had his father's total approval before he died, and that sealed the deal.

"This girl will make a good wife—she comes from a good family," his Papa once said to Pablo in his dying bed.

Pablo also knew his father wanted him to be happy in his life.

In early March of 1979, less than a year after his Papas death, Meky told Pablo she had heard that an evangelist by the name of Billy Graham was coming to Tampa.

"Billy who?" Pablo asked sarcastically.

"Billy Graham, a well-known world evangelist." she immediately responded.

Being a church girl she knew of Billy Graham, yet Pablo had never heard of him before. Pablo was a non-practicing Catholic and although he had been visiting Meky's Methodist Church, he couldn't care less about a bible thumping evangelist. As far as he was concerned the only evangelists he knew were those who held charismatic services in tents, with people screaming and fainting all over the place. Pablo didn't know who this Billy guy was, nor did he really care, life had battered him to the point, he had become somewhat cold and insensitive.

By that time, Pablo had been experimenting with drugs and alcohol. The last thing he needed was a preacher calling him out on the floor, revealing all the bad things he was doing. After much insisting from Meky, Pablo decided to please his young wife and go to the Crusade. Pablo's sister had also become interested in going, since she was dating a Christian boy at the time. When the Crusade finally got to Tampa Stadium, Pablo had already decided there was no way he was going to stay at the service for long. The way he figured it, going to the Crusade was a good opportunity to see the Tampa Bay Buccaneers Football Stadium for the first time.

As they approached the Stadium, Pablo noticed many of the people walking alongside of him were strangely joyful and exited to be there—nerds he thought.

Upon entering the football arena, and concerned that someone from the streets would recognize him at a religious event, Pablo told his wife he wanted to sit as far up in the stadium as possible. Once at the top seats of the *Big Sombrero*, as the stadium was known at the time, Pablo took more pleasure in sightseeing the surrounding area, than he did in what was actually happening on the grounds of the event.

After an hour of mind-numbing speakers and music, Pablo was ready to jump off from the top of the stadium, so he could end his misery. He then heard Billy Graham's name announced while the people roared. Interested in what the supposed well known preacher looked like; Pablo paid attention to Billy's introduction. Billy had been all over the world doing good and changing lives for the better. Pablo then listened with greater interest.

Shortly after the introduction, the well-known preacher stepped on to the platform on the grounds of the stadium, under an electrifying welcome roar of applause. Billy then smiled and waived his right hand to those in attendance. He then spoke with a peaceful tone of voice, "Hello and thank you Tampa, I come to you today in the name of our Lord and savior Jesus Christ."

The crowd roared again reminding Pablo of his childhood memories when he thought Fidel Castro had magical powers because the masses roared every time he spoke. This time it was different, this guy Billy was not like Fidel. There was a great difference between the two men from what Pablo could tell. One was humble and Godly—the other, proud and wicked.

When the crowds finally calmed down and Billy Graham began to preach, Pablo was impressed by his unassuming demeanor, so he listened with greater interest. Billy spoke with the conviction of someone who truly believed in what he was saying. Pablo also noticed the Billy wasn't overly animated—he didn't scream when he preached like other televangelist who appeared phony, making him feel uncomfortable.

The more Billy spoke, the more Pablo felt he was talking to him directly, taking him to an emotional place he had never been before. For a moment Pablo felt as if he was the only person in that stadium. It was like Billy had known all about Pablo's cultural machismo, and the self-protective wall he'd built around him to conceal his broken heart.

Like a windstorm, Billy continued to speak telling Pablo it was okay to feel the pain of sadness and disappointment, for God knew of all things and no matter how troubled a person is God loves him unconditionally. Feeling uneasy about all of the love talk, Pablo looked away hoping to hide the tears which slowly flooded his eyes. Worried about looking soft, he tried to hide his emotions from his young wife and others around him. For too long he had masked his feelings, having to be strong for his Mama and Sister, meanwhile dying inside.

His father's death had broken his heart beyond repair, and violence was the only way he knew to alleviate the all-encompassing pain. Suddenly and like a gentle breeze, the man they called Billy was telling Pablo about a love so strong nothing could ever break it. He also said to imagine heaven as a house with many rooms. A kingdom where there is no more pain and sorrow—a place unlike any other. As the service approached its ending, Billy asked a question no one had ever asked Pablo before.

"Do you know where you are going if you die today? Are you going to heaven or are you going to hell?" Billy asked.

Blown away by the straightforward question, Pablo's mind raced over the fact that he didn't have an answer to Billy's question. Overwhelmed with concern about not knowing where he was going if he died, Pablo struggled with his own emotions.

Shortly after that moment, Billy ended his message with an open invitation for those who wanted to accept Christ, as Savior and Lord. Suddenly, Pablo remembered the stories of those incarcerated men in Cuban prisons who were facing death by Castro's firing squads, and how they declared their faith in the Lord out loud before they died. Pablo also remembered the day his Papa accepted Christ as personal savior on his death bed, in the final hours of his life.

Billy continued speaking to Pablo's heart, "Come and let the love of God heal you of all of your pains." Billy said.   Overwhelmed by contradicting emotions, Pablo remained frozen in place, wondering what would become of him if he did die that day. He also wondered if this man Billy Graham was the real deal, or was he a snake oil salesman. Billy then spoke again; repeating his words about God's love.

Noticing the sea of people walking down the steps of the stadium, and on to the field below, while soft music played in the background; Pablo was moved to tears again. Once again concerned about appearing soft, he unsuccessfully tried to wipe the tears rolling down his face. The more he tried to restrain himself from following others to the field below, the louder his inner voice became. In his heart Pablo knew this was the one decision he desperately needed to make, yet, his hardened attitude of deep-rooted anger made him question his decision to go forward. He didn't want to do as hypocrites do; being good on Sundays in church and being like the devil the rest of the week. Pablo also thought of what others from the streets would think of him being in a religious gathering. Then it happened, Pablo lost himself in the moment and he stood tall, grabbed his young wife's hand and walked down the steps, and on to the stadium grounds. His sister and her boyfriend followed closely towards the stage where Billy stood with head bowed in prayer.

When at one point Pablo would have rather been getting root-canals, than to go to a religious event, he didn't regret the decision. On this cool April day in 1979, the gentle words of a Godly man known around the world as Billy, removed Pablo's hardened shield and led him in prayer to confess his sins and accept Christ into his heart, as Savior and Lord.

Drained from the emotions of the day, Pablo pondered over Billy's message. For the first time in his life, Pablo reflected on the significance of his own existence on this earth, as well as life ever after. Could he go to heaven with a hateful heart? He wondered. Pablo also wondered if God would understand the anger he felt against the man who he blamed for the sadness in his life. Not feeling worthy, Pablo also wondered if he belonged in heaven after all.

Although he tried to walk differently from that day on, Pablo's personal struggles continued. Yet, he knew that Billy's comforting words of an assured salvation in Christ appeased him. Although he was as flawed as any man, God's Grace was upon him.

"We are all a work in progress," Billy's words resonated in his head. "We've all sinned and fallen short of the Glory of God. We are all part of a falling world, yet our hope is in the Lord who died on the rugged cross, for you and for me."

Like a scratched vinyl album, Billy's words played in Pablo's head over and over again, "Listen son, we are all sinners. You can't save yourself of your imperfect ways. That is why you need Jesus." This is all you need to know, "For God so loved the world, He gave his one and only begotten Son, that whoever believes in him shall not perish but have eternal life. For God did not send his Son into the world to condemn the world, but to save the world through him. Whoever believes in him is not condemned, but whoever does not believe stands condemned already, because they have not believed in the name of God's one and only Son." Billy had touched Pablo's heart in a special way, even though the hatred against one man remained deeply engraved upon the wall of his heart.

Living in contradiction to his faith and while at church on Sunday, Pablo felt like an impostor, traveling in the fast lane of life, six days a week. Although the rebel in him had not subsided, he knew he'd been blessed with a good woman, who like Christ, offered him her unconditional love and the hope of raising a family of his own. Times had been hard for Pablo, but he had found a greater power than his own watching over him.

Chapter Four

1980

Almost a year to the date since the Billy Graham Crusade, Pablo turned on the radio on he's way home from work and heard an anti-Castro rally was being organized at a local park. By the time he arrived at local Park in West Tampa, hundreds of Cuban-Americans had already gathered with signs, flags and portable radios. By this time, they knew that on March 28, 1980 a young man by the name of Hector Sanyustiz acted on an escape plan he had been organizing secretly for months. Late that afternoon, one of the accomplices, a city bus driver by the name of Diaz Molina radioed his bosses. He told them one of his tires was dangerously low on air, and he needed to return to home base for repairs—he had lied. Instead, he let off the passengers and proceeded to pick up his four friends who were part of the plan, among them Sanyustiz and his 18-year-old stepson.

Before driving off, Diaz Molina stopped several blocks from Embassy Row in Havana. He dropped to his knees and asked everyone to pray for protection, the freedom mission was about to take place. Molina then turned the steering wheel over to Sanyustiz.

From what was heard at the park, Sanyustiz asked everyone to sit behind him and hold on tight, while Diaz Molina acted as a co-pilot on the front stairs of the bus. As they approached the Peruvian embassy, Sanyustiz picked up speed down the main avenue, made a sharp turn and plowed the bus through the embassy gates. Cuban Interior Ministry police guarding the embassy sprayed the bus with gunfire. Two bullets ripped into Sanyustiz—one in his left leg, the other in the right buttock. Gomez suffered superficial wounds in the head and back. A bullet killed one of the guards, a 27 year-old policeman. To create greater culpability against the youth, the Cuban government blamed the hijackers for the death of the government guard, but the

Peruvians embassy officials said one guards accidentally shot the other. Their report also indicated that the men on the bus weren't armed. The Cuban guards had shot their own man by mistake as they tried to gun down the occupants of the bus. Within minutes, the news about the young men crashing the bus had spread throughout the city; thousands of freedom seeking Cubans remained on high alert, as they hoped to also escape.

The backdrop of the harsh reality Sanyustiz and his friends faced in searching for freedom was that it was nearly impossible to get a visa to leave Cuba. Cubans had but two options to pursue freedom. One was to attempt escaping the heavily guarded coast lines of the island prison. Often doing so on man made rafts, tire inner tubes, and whatever floated, thus risking it all by attempting to cross the dangerous Florida straits. Their other option was to seek political asylum at a friendly embassy, protected by an agreement between Cuba and the friendly Latin American countries.

At a local park in Tampa, hundreds of people gathered in support of the uprising in Cuba. Folks anxiously listened to the incoming news on the radio from Miami. Although happy Sanyustiz and the others had successfully made it into the grounds of the Peruvian Embassy, the folks also knew of the wrath the young men could face if the Cuban government got their hands on them. They would have certainly faced life in prison, or death by firing squad.

As it turned out, the young men were granted formal amnesty, as Peruvian officials rushed Sanyustiz and Gomez to a Military Hospital in Havana to be treated for their wounds, the others remained in the Peruvian embassy. As hours passed, tension rose and relations between the two countries deteriorated. Cuba wanted the gate-crashers handed over for prosecution. The Peruvian Government refused the Cubans request.

Throughout Habana, mobs of government enticed supporters paraded through the streets chanting pro-government slogans and yelling profanities against Sanyustiz and the others. Many were throwing stones and eggs to at the Peruvian Embassy, demanding for the freedom seekers to be turned over to the mobs. The Communist tabloid Verde Olivo, *or* Olive Green, blared in bold headlines of the Communist controlled newspaper, referring to Sanyustiz and the others on the bus: '*Let others leave but not the murders! They will never leave alive!*'

Mobs were also posted outside the embassy clamoring Paredon, *or* to the firing wall! Above all they wanted Sanyustiz to be put before a firing squad. Upon hearing the news, Pablo became furthermore inspired by the courage of the young men. This was the time to act in support the events in Habana and spread the freedom spirit throughout Cuba.

The excitement of seeing the Miami and New Jersey rallies which were also organized to show support for the young men, energized the exiled anti-Castro commitment in

Tampa. The internal revolt in the island was precisely what many in the exiled community had been waiting for. The concurrent events in Havana revealed a crack in the armor of the Castro regime. For the first time in over twenty years of totalitarianism, the people of Cuba were showing open discontent, as they gathered outside the Peruvian Embassy in support of Sanyustiz and his group.

At the Tampa Park where the local community had gathered in support of the Cuban youth, everyone was buzzing with excitement. People wandered around trying to pick up any little tidbit of information they could. In the tumultuous gatherings Pablo noticed several men in camouflage uniforms—not American military, but irregulars, with patches on their upper arm. Pablo had never seen these men before. Suddenly, he realized who these stone face individuals were. Pablo remembered being warned to be on the lookout for these men—they were members of underground anti-Castro military group from Miami. Pablo looked up to these men with great respect; he knew they were the same men who had fought against Castro in the Escambray mountains of Cuba during the Cuban revolution. Pablo also knew that although many of those freedom fighters had died in their struggle; a few of the survivors were organized in the U.S exile and were ready to fight for the islands freedom once more.

After all of the excitement at the rally, there was no way Pablo could go back to work that day, it was too exciting, the passion for freedom had been reawakened. This time the world would know about the real Cuba and the crimes against humanity on the part of Castro's regime.

Pablo had chosen to never forget the fear and hunger of his childhood in Communist Cuba. The deaths of his Abuelo's back home and of his father in 1978, had pushed him further into depression and rambunctious behavior. He often thought of his best childhood friend Rolando, who had wanted to go to America more than anyone else. Yet, his opportunity to leave the country had passed and he had to enlist in the governments military. If he had been allowed to change his fate, Pablo was convinced that Rolando would have thrown caution to the wind and tried to escape Cuba, even if he died in the process. Ever since he could remember, Rolando had a clear vision of Pablo's future in America, but of his own future, he had seen nothing—he had no future to see. Rolando had been killed by a lightning strike, while boating on the Glorytown bay, shortly after Pablo had departed Cuba.

Pablo was married to a beautiful girl who was kind, sweet and patient with him, she was attending college studying to become a teacher and he was as supportive of her as he could possibly be. Part of him wanted to be the nice person who existed deep in his heart, yet he knew the truth about his uncontrollable anger. At times, others around him could feel the rage that emanated from his eyes, making

them nervous. Pablo didn't want to admit that to himself, it

would mean that he'd have to learn to put his anger aside and

walk away from it—he didn't want to do that. Instead, he

wanted to cultivate that anger and put it to use by settling the

score with his greatest menace, Fidel.

For years, it had been all Pablo thought about. Over

and over, he replayed in he's mind the thousand humiliations

and hardships the Communists had inflicted on him and his

family. Pablo cared nothing about himself—he could take

anything. The thought of his father's courage, enduring all

those years in the work camp made him more determined!

He often thought of his mama's sadness and mental fortitude

while her loving husband was gone. The way she maintained

her head up high, all the while forced to sell panatelas cakes

and durofrios, *or* flavored ice cubes on the black market to

feed his sister and himself! Pablo's memory of his Tio,

Uncle William's courage under pressure also played heavy

on his heart. William had his business nationalized and was sent to prison for false charges of crimes against the state. The vivid memory of his dear Abuela, being forced to wait in line for hours to get the miserable rationed portion of her family's food! Not to mention the humiliating name-calling, the intimidation, and the hunger for food. Sometimes Pablo felt so frustrated; he thought he would go crazy at any moment. The incident at the Peruvian embassy had ignited new hope for freedom outside, as well as within the island prison. Suddenly, life had taken a turn for the better—the spirit of revenge had been reawakened.

The next day, after finishing up at work, Pablo went back to the park. The size of the crowd had doubled. Opportunistic vendors were hawking food and drinks. People held candles and said prayers for the safety of the young men who had now officially been granted asylum by the Peruvians. This enraged Fidel to the point where he threatened to withdraw the guards from outside the embassy.

Thousands of Cubans had massed outside, and with no one to prevent them, they would flood the place. Nobody knew what the result of that would be, except that it would certainly be chaotic. More people might die. It could even lead to war.

For the next few days Pablo kept returning to the park. A number of his friends in their overflowing excitement sometimes stayed at the park overnight. While there, Pablo talked to as many people as he could let everyone know he and his family were ready to help in whatever way it was necessary. The news about the human dilemma in Cuba played day and night, therefore the entire Cuban community of Florida was on high alert, as it was elsewhere in America and the world.

That afternoon, one of the uniformed men approached Pablo at the park. The two had made eye contact with each other a number of times before, but concerned about the mysterious individual, Pablo remained at a distance—there was something frightening about him. The individual had beady eyes and he wore a permanent long scar on his face. He spoke with a rough tone voice, but that wasn't what concerned Pablo. Instead, it was the energy that radiated from him. This man had all the makings of an experienced hardened mercenary. Pablo just knew it; he could just smell the stench of violence in his demeanor.

Without preamble, he looked dead into Pablo's eyes and said, "Just think of all those poor people, crammed into that tiny space with no food or water."

"It's going to be bad," Pablo agreed, "sad isn't it? Those damn communist need to pay!"

The man nodded. "You know, there are a lot of people here in Florida wishing they could do something to get rid of Fidel."

"Well, I'm one of them," Pablo told the man.

"I thought so," he responded. "Where are you from?"

"Cienfuegos."

"Ah, yes, the Pearl of the South. What a beautiful city. Are you married?"

It struck him as an odd question. Pablo paused, the beady-eyed man waited for an answer.

"Yes."

"Any children?"

"Not yet."

"Do you have a job?"

Yes —Pablo responded concerned about all the questioning.

"Would anyone miss you if you were gone for a few weeks?"

Pablo then stared at him, uncomprehending at first. Then he realized what was happening. He was being recruited. But the question was, for what?

"They might miss me" he responded cautiously. "But there's ways around that."

"I see." The man nodded. "Will you be here tomorrow?"

"Yes."

"Fine, meet me here at one.

By the way, what is your name?" Pablo asked the mysterious man.

"My name is. . . Punson," said the man. "Major Punson that is! That is what you will call me from now on. *Me Entiendes or* Understand?"

"Yes."

"Don't tell anyone that we've been talking. Not your wife, nobody. Is that clear?"

"Yes, Sir."

"Fine."

And with that, Punson melted into the crowd.

Pablo could hardly sleep again that night. He and his wife lived in government-subsidized housing, and it was hot in those apartment blocks—hot and loud. But that didn't bother him. Pablo had been raised under the hot Cuban sun in his hometown of Glorytown, after all.

No matter how much Pablo tried to avoid thinking of Punson, thoughts drifted to Punson all night long. Pablo assumed based on his age and other clues, Punson somehow must have been involved with the Bay of Pigs Invasion in 1961—a mercenary. As an anti-Castro and fellow Cuban, Pablo knew Punson was committed to the cause of overthrowing Fidel. But what did he really want? What could Pablo hope to offer? True, he was young and fit—he ran several miles a day—and was full of anger. But he had no military training, no money, nothing he could use. Pablo was just another angry young man. Realistically, what was he going to do—stab Fidel with his pocket knife?

Well, of course he thought Punson already knew that, yet he wanted to talk to Pablo anyway. Was he being played for a fool, or could this be the opportunity Pablo had dreamed about ever since he left the island prison?

Shortly after the anti-Castro rally had ended the next day, Felix, the event organizer asked to meet Pablo in an isolated area of the park where they had been gathered. Walking in darkness, Punson and a stranger followed them to a dark place away from the crowd. At first, Pablo thought the meeting was drug related, common during that period of time. Having no personal interest in dealing drugs, Pablo guardedly complied and then he saw the stranger's face. He was someone he knew, but whose face he couldn't place. Then he remembered him from a recent Miami newspaper article; he was one of the leaders in the militant anti-Castro underground society in Miami and New Jersey.

"Mi nombre es Santiago, come estas?" *or* "My name is Santiago, how are you?"

"Bien, gracias, *or* well gracias" Pablo responded.

"Are you Cuban?"

Yes Sir I am."

"I understand you want to free our people from tyranny?"

Not knowing the purpose of the meeting, Pablo remained quiet for a moment; he then spoke with a thousand thoughts rising in his mind.

"Who wants to know?" Pablo asked suspiciously while looking intensely in his eyes.

Santiago smiled as to be pleased with Pablo's brash attitude. He then proceeded to convey the message he had traveled 250 miles from Miami to deliver.

"I want to offer you an opportunity of a lifetime. Are you interested?"

"It depends." Pablo then cautiously agreed to listen. After an hour conversation, the two came to an agreement. Pablo was to meet him in the Everglades two weeks later to begin sniper training. The mission, infiltrate the island prison of Cuba and permanently silence the voice of the bearded bastard, as Fidel was referred to among those who wanted him dead.

"Before Pablo had to leave the meeting," Santiago said, "I want to make sure you understand the seriousness of this undertaking. You are Pablo; answering to any other name could jeopardize the security of the attempt. *M'entiendes?*"

"I do" Pablo responded

"You also understand that you must be ready for anything... including death. But worse than death is torture. There is no way to prepare for torture, and everyone breaks at some point. Do I have to worry about that with you?"

"You should know better than to ask that question. I wouldn't be here if I was soft." Pablo responded with the sound of strong conviction in his voice.

"OK, good! I only mention it because I want there to be no doubt about this matter."

"You must understand that if you are caught, the U.S. government won't acknowledge you and neither will we. The Cubans won't exactly welcome you with open arms; they will mercilessly look to break you down for information. On our end, we promise to do everything we can to free you from any prison they take you. Of course there is a good possibility they will kill you if you don't talk. *M'entiendes?*" Santiago asked with a steely gaze.

"Are you serious about this?" Pablo asked in disbelieve.

Santiago fixed his eyes on me with a steely gaze.

"I am always serious when it comes to freeing my people. So let that be the last time you ever ask me such a question."

Pablo stared at him and nodded in agreement.

"Before we do anything," he followed. "You must continue to do high cardio physical conditioning and mental strength training of your own. I want to make sure you are

77

well prepared for strenuous journey. A man by the name of Ramon will be taking you to Miami, then to a clandestine training camp in the Everglades as soon as possible. Don't breathe a word of this to anyone. Tell your friends and family whatever you have to, but don't make them suspicious. I will assign a person by the name of Jorge to be our P.R. man in the States. We need someone to speak to the media after we are successful so your identity is protected. And I mean WE WILL be successful!" You have been destined for this moment boy—think you can handle it?"

For a moment Pablo wondered if Punson had made a mistake referring him to Santiago. Maybe he thought it was someone else. But he didn't appear to be the kind of man who makes rash decisions or judge someone incorrectly. If he thought Pablo had leadership potential, then this meant Pablo would not disappoint him.

"Of course I can handle it," Pablo responded assertively.

"Good. Now, let's talk about the plan."

Santiago and Pablo spent the rest of the afternoon going over the basics of the mission. "We are going to charter a fishing boat out of the Key West. A boat captain will be waiting for you on the dock. You will carry no guns and no identification. This must appear to be a fishing trip— Jorge and I will remain here in Tampa to support your family and to contact them if you perished or are imprisoned. *Me Entiendes?*" Santiago asked firmly.

"The trip to Cuba will go as follows; you will head west in the Gulf of Mexico, then south between the Yucatan Peninsula and Cuba's westernmost point. Your immediate destination is the Old Man Bay on the north coast of the Cayman Islands. Once there, you will wait for word to double back and head north towards Cuba's southern city of Trinidad. You will land at night, a man known as Raton *or* the mouse, will be waiting for you on the coastline. He is a member of a rebel resistance group in the region. He will take over the mission from there; Raton is one of us, you can trust him! He will take you to a safe house outside of Trinidad where weapons and ammunition will be waiting for you. Once there you will wait for orders from us. *Me Entiendes?*"

According to intelligence sources in Cuba, Fidel had a mistress by the name of Dalia Gomez Del Valle who lives in Trinidad, a place Fidel visits often and the locals knew it. The latest news was that he would be on his way to Dalia's home soon to avoid the troubles in Havana. Once we know of the exact timing of the visit, you will be taken to the location where you will deliver his medication. *Me Entiendes?*"

In his heart Pablo knew this attempt was extremely dangerous and although he was concerned, he didn't want to back out. He'd been angry at Fidel for a long time, yet the seriousness of the attempt concerned him. Then Punson told Pablo he would be in contact when it was time for the next phase.

"Be ready," he said.

Having heard all he needed to hear, Pablo headed for the door then Punson grabbed his arm, looked him in the eyes and said, "Listen, I've been watching you for the last few days in the park, looking for a weakness."

"Really!" Pablo responded dismissively. "And why is that?"

"Because you go around with fire in your eyes, as if you harbor hatred and pain. You reminded me of when I was young, full of piss and vinegar—like a nuclear bomb always about to go off. You stick out like a sore thumb to someone like me. I know a fighter when I see one. I tell you this only because I am never wrong about people, and I know you have what it takes to succeed with this job."

"What are you going to tell your family?"

"I don't know yet," Pablo responded. "I'll think of something. Maybe I will tell them I am going to New York City on business"

"Will they buy it?"

Pablo shrugged. "They'll have to," he said.

"You might be gone for weeks. Months, even."

"That's a risk I'm prepared to take," Pablo responded"

"Whatever you do," Punson warned, "you don't breathe a word of this to anyone."

"Of course not, you can trust me. Now let go of my arm."

"I trust you," said Punson, releasing Pablo.

He wasn't sure who Punson was, never having seen him before Pablo didn't fully trust him, but he certainly sensed the man had important connections. Everyone knew the CIA was behind the exiled Cubans in the Bay of Pigs invasion. Punson had dropped enough hints to confirm that he had been involved. Yet, Pablo also remembered there had been many questions surrounding Kennedy's assassination, and what role the CIA, Castro or even the Mafia, might have played in it—which was both reprehensible and blood-chilling. Pablo was worried that the CIA might be involved in this operation and that they would botch it as badly as they had botched the Bay of Pigs invasion, as well as other attempts on Castro. The gossip was that certain Mafia families, of which there were many in Tampa, wanted Castro gone, too. Not out of any moral conviction, but because he had liquidated all foreign business interests on the island, including theirs, and they were still upset about it. A Cuba without Castro held great money-making potential for them.

Pablo certainly wanted nothing to do with those kinds of people. He had his own reasons for wanting to get to Castro. Naturally, so did lots of others. According to some stories going around in the Cuban community, there had been over six hundred attempts on Castro's life so far, all ending in failure. But not this time, Pablo and his team didn't intend to fail this time. They were determined to go down in history as the men who finally pulled off what so many others had tried to do in vain.

Then it happened. Angry at the Peruvians, on April 4, Castro ordered the removal of his military guards from the Peruvian embassy on Good Friday. When word spread throughout Havana, people flocked to the embassy. By Saturday, the freedom seekers had grown to more than 300. By nightfall, it was thousands. On Easter Sunday, more than 10,800 people were jammed into the grounds, clamoring for political asylum.

Suddenly, this had become a human dilemma of gigantic proportions. The embassy refugees had found a way to send messages to President Carter, Pope Paul II and other heads of state requesting assistance in leaving Cuba. Seeing the potential for human disaster, Fidel Castro makes an impromptu visit to the vicinity of Peruvian Embassy to observe the refugee situation.

In Tampa, the group knew all the stars appeared to lining up in our favor, as the United States military announced exercises to be carried out in the US and the naval base at Guantanamo. While in Habana, anti U.S. demonstrations were staged two blocks from the U.S. Interest Section. "Yankee Go Home" slogans were shouted. If intelligence served us right, soon the bastard would be on his way to his hideaway in the Trinidad Mountains.

Then began the waiting game—not just for Pablo, but for all Cubans in Tampa and elsewhere anxious to see what would happen in Habana. Pablo was suffering two kinds of suspense: one concerning the impending mission, the other, the fate of the people trapped in the Peruvian Embassy which could influence our attack.

Every day, Pablo and the others went back to park hoping to get word from Punson. A crowd would gather regularly to exchange information and wait for news. A week had passed and the refugees had been reduced to eating the leaves and bark off the trees within the embassy compound. They were also drinking their own urine. It was already a human catastrophe, and it had the potential to become a humanitarian disaster. The regime knew the world was now watching as were the millions of Cubans in the island who were watching the oppressive regime closely for a weakness. By 1980 and 11 years of broken promises, the people of Cuba knew Castro was an incompetent dictator who ruled with an iron fist, and communism was a lie. The slightest slip of the government's stronghold could start a revolution.

As pressure mounted on the regime, on April 20, 1980, a frustrated Fidel Castro proclaimed in Habana that any Cuban who wished to immigrate to the United States could board a boat at the nearby port of Mariel, included among them, the Peruvian Embassy refugees. During the ensuing months, some 125,000 Cubans fled to Florida in about 1,700 packed boats, at times overwhelming the U.S. Coast Guard and immigration authorities. The situation had created a political crisis for President Jimmy Carter. It turned out that some of the exiles had been released from Cuban jails and mental health facilities. Castro had it all well calculated; why not dump the problem on America!

This was the time to strike and the team knew it. Somehow they had to find a way by which to infiltrate the island prison and get in position for the attack. The problem was going to be navigating around the madness of the freedom flotilla which was heavily supervised by the US Coast Guard. Shortly after, Pablo received a message from Punson, the time had come for the final preparations; Pablo was to study a map of the Trinidad area until he knew it like the back of his hand. But most importantly, Pablo was to go over the different strategies of the operation until he knew it in his sleep. He intensified his physical training regimen until he lost every ounce of fat he had on him. Pablo had been selected by Punson, to be the trigger man.

Nothing had ever prepared him for a moment like this. Pablo honestly knew he wasn't a killer; in fact he was a good hearted person. His dilemma was that he knew Castro was not good and Communism was not a good thing!

At night, these contradicting thoughts robbed Pablo of his sleep and in the day, he thought of them again, oftentimes not focusing on his work. Pablo wondered what his family and friends would think if they knew of my involvement with an assassination attempt. Not to speak of what Billy would say, above all he wondered what God would say. Could he find a way to understand my point of view? He don't think so, were his thoughts—no one understood.

And so Pablo moved forward with the plans he had given his word to uphold. Nothing could stop him now. Too much had happened. He was damaged goods and there was only one way to resolve his problems—revenge. For too many years the only way he could sleep was by envisioning himself standing unremorsefully over Fidel's lifeless body lying in a pool of blood. And so when it came time to sleep at night, Pablo's turbulent thought of murdering someone often kept him awake all nigh, The only thing that brought him relieve, was the ever-present thought of accomplishing his mission. El Salmon y su corrida de libertad! The Salmon and its run to freedom—and so he dreamed.....

Chapter Five

The Salmon Run

A quiet self-confident man drove him to Key West from Miami shortly after Pablo had completed his sniper training in the Everglades and then one final meeting in the city of Hialeah.

"My name is Ramón," he said in broken English, "don't ask me any questions; I am only your driver." he stated firmly.

"Yes Sir!" Pablo responded without hesitation.

Ramón didn't know that Pablo had already read his full profile in Tampa and by now knew all about him. Pablo knew the one thing that most didn't—Ramón was in fact a very dangerous man and the mastermind behind the attack on Fidel. The instruction given to Pablo on how to deal with Ramón were simple, do not speak to him unless you are spoken to.

As a lifelong hit man, Ramón didn't trust many people, he most likely didn't trust Pablo either, yet Ramon's calm demeanor revealed a sense of respect for the young man. A tall handsome Cuban man with red toned-hair and green eyes, Ramon could easily pass for an American. He was a high-ranking member of an underground anti-Castro militant group based in south Florida and New Jersey. The word on him was that he was as cold blooded a killer as you could find, and would do whatever it took to achieve the ultimate goal of silencing Castro's voice forever.

Ramón had once been an explosives expert with the rebel army that fought Castro in the early days of the revolution in Cuba. He had also fought daringly in the Bay of Pigs invasion, later becoming an intelligence operative with close ties to the CIA. Ramón also had other credentials in his underground world resume; he had spent time in Dallas in the fall of 1963. Although only a few knew of his presence there, some associated Ramón with a man standing on the grassy knoll of Dealey Plaza holding a black umbrella on the morning of November 22.

Ramón was never implicated in the death of the American President, yet whenever someone spoke of Lee Harvey Oswald in Ramón's presence, his facial demeanor changed for the worse. Ramón considered Oswald a wannabe and the Warren Commission, a political farce.

He was a solitary man who lived hidden in the shadows of the anti-Castro underworld. His only significance for living revolved around liberating Cuba from the Communist and he knew the only way to accomplish that was to kill the leader. In Pablo's eyes, anyone who hated Castro that much was trustworthy. Although Pablo was not associated with any anti-Castro political group or the CIA, he knew that to succeed in the attack, he needed knowledgeable support from Ramón, who because of his age proffered to mastermind the attack.

The two didn't speak again for the rest of the trip as Pablo's mind drifted in and out of shallow sleep, noticing Ramón's heavy glance from time to time. His face mysteriously revealed by the dashboard lights.

Upon arrival in Key West, Ramón drove Pablo to a remote area for two weeks of training. After the training, Ramón drove him to an isolated place by the sea where a boat awaited in solitude. "*Mira allí, ese es Manolo*, Look over there that's Manolo," said Ramón, signaling with his eyes towards a dark figure standing at the end of the dock in the midst of a heavy fog.

"*Escucha*, Listen," he said lightly extending his arm towards Pablo with a note.

"Give this to Manolo; he will take over from here." he added.

He then took Pablo's other hand and placed a rifle bullet in it.

"Go on and give my best to that bearded bastard." he said in a calm firm voice, while looking fervently into Pablo's eyes.

"Make us proud young man." he said, then turned and walked away.

Pablo stood still, looking at Ramon as he walked away disappearing into the fog. He then turned and looked at Manolo's figure standing motionless at the end of the dock.

Pablo remained standing still in the eerie stillness of the silent fog. Then a chilling thought occurred to him, he was dealing with trained assassins who could choose to silence him if he did not go through the plan. Pablo then heard his father's voice in his mind reminding him that only cowards walk away from duty. Knowing he was no coward, Pablo placed Ramón's bullet in his front coat pocket, then proceeded to walk down the screechy old fishing dock, in the gloomy silence of a thick, wet April fog. Firmly walking towards the figure, Pablo's mind raced in every direction, his heart beat uncontrollably with every step he took as sweat poured down his face. Like a dream, everything appeared magnified under the watchful eyes of resting pelicans.

The closer Pablo got to the figure, the faster his heart pounded in his chest. Then, he felt a spine-chilling mixture of dread and peace. Suspended by the unyielding fog, Pablo looked down at his legs wondering what was wrong. When at one point along the way he had been fully aware of his body movements, feeling his legs sturdily underneath him, he now felt frozen in time, immobilized by the fear of the uncertain. He then looked up and the dark figure of a man at the end of the dock appeared further away than before. Pablo had only heard about what paralyzing fear could do to a man, now he knew! Then, he looked up and there before him was Manolo. The sturdy old man of the sea stood motionless in his space, his legs spread wide, like a fearless warrior. He proudly wore his well-combed snow-white hair like a crown, his face, a road map of deep wrinkled mess.

Manolo remained motionless, his hands resting confidently in the front pockets of his weathered faded black raincoat and an uncompromising look of conviction in his sea blue eyes. He pulled his right hand out of his coat slowly then reached out to Pablo with a metal rigid handshake.

"Bienvenido, yo soy Manolo, sígueme" "Welcome, I am Manolo, follow me." he said in a serene, bottomless voice.

Without saying another word, he led Pablo on board his fishing vessel named Lucia. Pablo guardedly complied knowing that once he stepped inside of the boat, there was no turning back to the life he had known as his own. When at one point along the way he had seen his legs moving, this time he looked and they were ice blocks, frozen stiff. The lifelong desire to end his tormenting anger against Fidel had arrived. Although Pablo trusted God was with him, he couldn't avoid thinking of how He could approve of killing. In his heart Pablo related killing Castro to killing a roach; no one misses a roach he thought. Hoping God would understand, In Pablo's mind this was duty and the only place he was going was south.

"Relax, son, we have a long journey ahead." said Manolo gently while interrupting Pablo's thoughts.

Unable to restrain his curiosity any longer, Pablo decided to ask Manolo about the bearded bastard name Ramon had given Fidel.

"Sir, can you please tell me why Ramón calls Fidel, the Bearded Bastard?"

Manolo grinned and immediately took the cigar out of his mouth.

"It is said that Fidel's father, Angel Castro was an immigrant from Spain who had prospered in Cuba as a sugarcane farmer and land thief. Although Castro's father was married, he had five children out of wedlock with his maid, Lina Ruz González—Fidel was one of the five kids. Although years later, Angel and Lina formalized their relationship and married, to us, Fidel remains a bastard child."

Satisfied with Manolo's clarification, Pablo smiled. Also intrigued by the name on the back side of Manolo's boat, Pablo then asked, Manolo about the name Lucia.

Manolo paused, and then glanced at him briefly as to question Pablo's curiosity; he then turned his head away towards the horizon as to purposely conceal the emotion in his eyes. Turning back facing Pablo, he pointed towards the back of the boat and said "Put your belongings underneath that seat then come back up front." Pablo complied and returned to the old mans side hoping to hear his answer, but Manolo remained thoughtfully quiet.

Pablo didn't take Manolo's silence personal as he went about the business of starting the boat engines. Perhaps he shouldn't have asked Manolo anything about his personal life Pablo thought, yet he desperately needed to know about the man he had entrusted with his life.

After a lengthy period of silence, Manolo spoke again.

"Why are you so interested in the name boy?" The old man asked.

"I don't know sir; it's just that Lucia is a beautiful name."

Looking at him again with a delayed frozen stare, Manolo began to speak.

"Lucia was my wife." he said while removing the boat rope from the old wooden pillars.

"She died a few years ago."

"May I ask how she died, Sir?"

Pausing once again, Manolo then said, "She died of..."

"What do you mean, Sir?" Pablo persisted.

"She died of a broken heart son. Once upon a time…
when we were both young and deeply in love," he said.
"Lucia and I were part of a group of student activist writers
at the University of Havana. Soon after Castro's take over,
we noticed how the new government was beginning to
control our freedom of expression. They especially did not
like us questioning their authority through our independent
writing. In essence, we were questioning the political course
of the newly established administration. A group of us then
decided to organize a peaceful demonstration in the streets
around the capitol in Havana. We were protesting the
governments crack down on freedom of the press. You were
too young to remember those days son, but since you asked,
I will finish my story if it's okay with you?"

"Absolutely it is Sir, please go on!" Pablo insisted.

Glancing at the inquisitive young man briefly as to
look for signs of genuine interest, Manolo then continued
with his narrative.

"One of the first things the Castro regime did when it took over power in Cuba was to eliminate the freedom of expression thus terminating free press. In 1965 the new government published their own newspaper called El Granma, which was in fact the Communist Central Committee's way to brainwash the people. We were young and naive, so we stood against the new government policies" he said shaking his head lightly, and then stopped talking.

As Manolo steered the boat slowly out of the foggy cove, he turned away from Pablo, his figure vanishing briefly in the fog. Pablo had obviously hit a sensitive note with the old man and he wasn't about to let it go. He needed to know if Manolo's hatred for Castro ran as deep as Ramón's did. After a few minutes, Manolo reappeared from the fog running his rugged, wrinkled hands across his face. He then spoke again. "Come closer to me son," he requested. "It's important that I finish answering your question."

Pablo stood next to him close enough to smell tobacco in his breath. Manolo was a stranger, yet he felt appeased in his presence. Perhaps it was because Manolo reminded him of the men who had influence his young life—quiet and strong men like his Father and Grandfather.

While Pablo waited for the old man to go on with the story, Pablo's mind drifted briefly. Looking across the mystifying sea with puzzling anticipation not knowing what awaited him on the other side of the journey, Pablo remained quiet.

As the boat reached maximum speed, the young man glanced at Manolo from the side of his eyes hoping he wouldn't notice. The old man stood tall and self-assured. With his white hair flying in the wind, Manolo stood focused on the sea ahead, knowing of its fickle ways. As the vessel ripped through the deep ocean waves periodically thrashing the Lucia on the water like a toy, Manolo appeared content. It soon became clear to Pablo that the old man was at peace in his environment. The open sea was the only place where he truly felt connected to Lucia and free. His love for every living organism in the deep blue waters of the Gulf was obvious, as was his contagious serenity.

Pablo's trust in Manolo was growing with every ocean mile they traveled. The old man's heart and his own were connecting in a common purpose.

After a long pause of silence, Manolo finally decided to finish speaking about Lucia. Looking at Pablo for a moment while removing his windblown hair from his face, Manolo spoke again. "Soon after the government had begun cracking down on all journalists; Lucia and I went underground and continued to write about our discontent with Castro's revolution. There were too many promises unmet. Eventually I was arrested and slapped with a twenty year prison sentence for committing crimes against the state through my writing.

Without public knowledge, the laws of the land had changed and since I was denied legal representation, I began to serve my sentence immediately."

"What about Lucia?" Pablo asked.

Manolo's eyes grew misty as he took a deep breath fighting back the tears of his broken heart. With emotion in his voice, he then continued. "Lucia served a couple of months in jail for being my accomplice. Upon her release she fought for my freedom as long as she could. She wrote letters to international newspapers and heads of states all over the world, but no one responded. Seeing the futility of her efforts, she went into a deep depression and took her own life three years into my sentence. In the last letter she wrote me, she said that she could no longer live without me." The old man solemnly concluded while wiping the tears off his face.

Deeply moved by then, Manolo asked Pablo to take over the steering of the vessel—he then turned and walked away. His silence spoke volumes to the seriousness of the

mission. Its reality became more evident as the craft steadily

separated the two from U.S territory. They were now alone

in pursuing their long awaited goal of silencing the bastard's

voice once and for all.

Manolo's purpose had become additionally clear to

Pablo; the old man wanted revenge just as badly as he did.

The assignment was to infiltrate the heavily guarded island

of Cuba and conduct a sniper attack on the one who was to

blame for the pain of millions—Fidel Castro.

In line with Ramón's orders, the mission was to be

disguised as a fishing expedition, departing from Key West

to the north coast of the Cayman Islands, through The

Yucatan Channel. Once there, the final arrangements would

be made to enter Cuba through the Southern coast, near the

Bay of Pigs area. They didn't take any firearms on the trip in

the event that U.S or Cuban Coast Guards would stop and

search them along the way. They carried only fishing equipment and bait to disguise themselves as fishermen. Only Ramón's bullet served as an invariable reminder of the seriousness of the mission. The sniper rifle, along with other weapons had already been smuggled onto the Island days earlier and they were now in the possession of the anti-Castro commandos supporting the attack in the island. These individuals were mostly aged insurrectional rebels who fought against Fidel and were sentenced to long prison terms. All of them lived or had relocated to the mountains around the aged colonial city of Trinidad.

This group of men and women rebels had been chasing the elusive dream of liberating Cuba from oppression by the Castro regime since it took power. Although much older now and physically limited, they were glad to help in carrying out the attack.

As informed earlier, Trinidad was the location where Castro's Mistress, Delia Soto Del Valle was originally from and where she and Fidel had a home. Delia had raised their five children there while Fidel remained in Havana, only going to his mountainside hideaway periodically according to the commando's intelligence. This was to be the location of the attack on the bearded bastard, Fidel. Pablo, along with an accomplice, would make their way to the underground hideaway where Pablo would live for days. The mountainside grotto had been strategically dug-up to overlook Dalia's home below. This was to be the one shot that would change the course of history for ever.

Pablo knew that there had been many sophisticated CIA attempts on Castro's life in the past, but the lack of sophistication of their practical plan encouraged him. He didn't see Manolo for a while on the boat; all he saw were the blue ocean and the sea gulls and dolphins dancing in the waves. Then within the turbulent skies he saw his own life flash in front of him like a dream. He saw snap shots of happier days on San Carlos Street with his Abuelo's standing on their front porch. He saw his friends, Tito and Rolando running free in those glorious childhood days under the sun. Then suddenly, their figures disappeared and all he could see was infinite sea waltzing with the sky in the far horizon, while the sun peaked playfully over the Gulf of Mexico, while chasing the fog away.

Manolo then tapped Pablo on the shoulder gently, directing his sight to the other side of the boat and towards their final destination. This was the one place they loved more than any other. The place which in their minds entrapped the lost years of the youth that never was.

The further south they traveled, the closer Cuba appeared to be, looking reachable with a stone with its green mountains disappearing into the blue-green waters of the forbidden tropical paradise. After a few hours and well into their journey,

Manolo's deep voice sounded off again like thunder in the wind, breaking the dreadful and unrelenting sound of power engines.

"Mira ayí! Look directly ahead boy!" he said.

"That's the Cayman Islands in the distance, we will soon be there."

Pablo looked and nodded in affirmation, he then drifted off again into his own anxious mind—he knew the time of truth was soon approaching. As they approached land, Manolo turned the powerful twin engines off. He then looked at Pablo and signaled for him to remain quiet while they drifted in the soft current that ran along the marshland of the northern Grand Cayman coastline. The sun now faded behind them as did the ever-present sound of the seagulls.

Manolo appeared to be looking for an isolated place on the coastline, a place called Bahia del Viejo or Old Man Bay he would later say. This had been the location previously arranged with a support team of the operation.

They were to provide vital information for the final part of the trip as well as much needed fuel.

Manolo had been at Old Man Bay before; Pablo could tell by the calm in his well trained ocean eyes as well as his relaxed posture.

"Get ready to drop anchor boy, this is where we will sleep tonight. We will head north from here in the morning."

"Why this place Manolo?"

"Well," calmly said the old man, "Bahia del Viejo has been a lucky place for me. I feel safe and lucky here."

"What does that mean sir?"

"I mean fishing lucky," he said with a grin on his face. "You see boy, I know these waters like I know myself. Out of all of the places I have dropped anchor in my life; the outer reef of El Viejo is the best fishing spots in the World by far!" Pablo nodded satisfied with Manolo's answer knowing there was more to it.

Once the anchor was set, the old man released the steering wheel and walked away from it while rubbing his cramping fingers together, slowly making his way to the front of the boat where the sun was setting. He then stopped at point's edge. Standing tall on the hull of his old faithful Lucia, he calmly reached into the inside pocket of his rugged old coat and pulled out a large cigar, then lit it. Pablo waited observantly in silence thinking that perhaps this was the old man's secret war ritual performed in the creepy silence of El Viejo Bay with soft waves gently rocking the Lucia.

Inhaling deeply the sweet smoke of his Cuban cigar, Manolo was finally relaxed for the first time since they had left Key West. He then opened his arms wide like a seabird in the sky, tilted his head back and took a deep breath, while his long black coat and silky white hair danced freely in the wind. Manolo stood motionless for a while as if to wait for approval from above. Then he let the smoky air out of his lungs, turned and stared at Pablo momentarily, then spoke.

"You like fishing boy?"

"Could live without it, sir" Pablo answered cautiously.

"Do you know about the Salmon boy?"

"No, Sir, not particularly," Pablo responded without delay hoping to promote the old man's explanation.

"You're like the Salmon boy." Manolo said peacefully as darkness quickly came upon them. Not knowing what to say, Pablo remained quiet, once again, hoping the old man clarified his point. He then continued.

"You see boy, you have been chosen to return to your natal stream like the Salmon."

"I don't understand! What are you trying to say, sir?" Pablo asked guardedly. In the cool breeze of the old bay with only the full moon as their witness, Pablo waited in silence for Manolo to respond. Somehow, he knew the old man desperately wanted him to understand the fundamental value of their mission; Pablo knew there was no room for error if they were going to succeed in attempt, so he listened carefully.

Manolo then spoke again. "The Pacific Salmon is an amazing fish you know—when they reach sexual maturity they return to their natal streams. They make the trip only once in their lifetime as they swim hundreds, even thousands of miles to get back to the stream where they were born. Even though a small percentage of Salmon live to reach their natal spawning grounds, they all make the rigorous journey. Most of them die, only the strong survive and make it to their spawning streams."

The old man then stopped and looked at Pablo to make sure he was listening. Pablo looked at him in the eyes boldly, revealing greater interest. The old man then continued.

"The females will fight females for places to nest and the males fight other males for the available females. The process continues until all the eggs and sperm have been deposited. The Pacific Salmon then die within a few days of spawning." The old man paused for a moment, as if to allow Pablo to comprehend the message he was conveying. He then continued.

"You see what I mean now boy?" Manolo asked.

Pablo didn't respond he just nodded in affirmation as Manolo proceeded.

"You see boy…you are the Salmon!"

"What are you trying to say, sir?" Pablo asked mystified as the southeast winds intensified.

Manolo didn't reply, he turned his head north towards Cuba and puffed on his cigar once more. Then within a cloud of white smoke, he raised his right hand pointing north.

"That's the way to your natal stream son. You are going back to fertilize the eggs of hope and freedom for the next generation. Whether you succeed in killing the bastard or not, the next generation of Cubans will always remember you for having had the courage to return to the place where you were born and spawn so they could live in peace. Do you understand now son? You are the Salmon and this is your run!"

Manolo waited briefly for Pablo's reaction, but all he heard was the sound of the sea. Convinced that Pablo had understood his message; Manolo turned and walked away. In the silence of night, everything around appeared magnified to Pablo. In that moment his whole life appeared before his eyes, like a movie at the Jagua Theater on San Carlos Street. The more he thought about those special moments in the cradle of his childhood—the greater the passion for Cuba's freedom became.

He and Manolo didn't speak again that night—there was no need. The Salmon Run was on.

Chapter Six

Cuban Territory

By 3:00 AM the next morning and after meeting with their associates, Manolo and Pablo left Old Man Bay and headed north towards their final destination. Although not a word was spoken early on, the two remained visually connected. At one point Manolo turned to Pablo who stood vigilantly to the right of the old warrior and winked as if to say, relax boy, everything is going to be all right. Looking north while distancing themselves from Old Man Bay, the old man looked at home in the darkness of the night filled with nocturnal undercurrents. The focused look in his eyes defined the endorphin producing excitement only cold blooded killers on a mission could understand. Manolo was one of those; Pablo was soon becoming one of them. In only minutes, the two would be in Cuban waters, then on land to meet their guide as previously planned.

After a long time of silence Manolo spoke, *"Cielo empedrado - suelo mojado"*

"What does that mean Sir?"

"Stony sky—soaked soil," Manolo said pointing to the sky. "When you see stone like clouds in the darkness of the night instead of stars, it doesn't mean that the stars aren't there, they are just hidden by the clouds which promise rain."

"This was the plan wasn't it Sir—rain?"

"Glad to see you are finally catching on boy!"

"Yes, this was indeed the plan. Rain means the Coast Guard is less likely to be out on patrol. Pray for rain boy and be ready to hold on, you are going for the ride of your life!"

Not knowing exactly what Manolo meant, Pablo grabbed the front railing of the craft. Manolo went silent again, with only a grin on his wrinkled face. He then opened the Lucia's twin engines to full throttle turning it into a space rocket softly kissing the surface of the water. This was the moment of truth and there was no room for hesitation. As if to proclaim his space within the sea, Manolo speared the Lucia into the dark horizon with reckless abandon. It was obvious he had traveled the waters of the Caribbean Sea before and once again he was claiming his place.

Soon the Lucia entered into Cuban waters. Manolo cut the engines off as if to clear his mind and listen for familiar sounds.

"What do you expect to hear Sir?"

"I have no expectations son, only knowledge"

"With all do respect Sir, what do you mean?"

"Look boy!" He said pointing to the north sky. "That is a storm coming from the top of the *Escambray Sierra Mountains*; I am listening for the far rumble of clouds. I smell the sweet fragrance of Liberty in its wind. The storm will soon be upon us, so prepare yourself for the sea dance boy, Cuba awaits us!" Manolo said serenely while looking at the sea. He then walked to the back of the boat and grabbed two rain coats from a compartment where he also kept his fishing gear.

"It looks like the stars are lining up for us tonight boy."

"What stars Sir? I see nothing but black skies above."

"Like I told you before, they are there, but you must first believe!"

Pablo didn't respond he just looked at the old man hoping the rain storm would pass by quickly so he could take off the old bait smelling raincoat Manolo had given him. Not being in the proper state of mind and feeling he had already tested Manolo's patience with too many questions. Pablo quietly prepared for the unpredictable storm ahead trusting Manolo's knowledge of the stars and the sea.

As the old man had predicted, the rain came down like darts from an angry sky. Within seconds the Lucia was engulfed by the blinding torrential rain common in the

Caribbean Sea. The old man started up the engines and full throttled it again towards the southern Cuban coast knowing the storm would muffle the sound of its powerful engines. '*He must be crazy*' Pablo thought as the Lucia pounced on the rough surface of the choppy sea with fearless conviction. This was the time to advance and Manolo knew it; surely Castro's Coast Guard wouldn't be so crazy as to be out on the open sea at a time like this.

By four in the morning, the storm had passed and the gray silhouette of the Escambray Mountains appeared to the west. These were the same mountains Pablo remembered from happier childhood day when he rode on the gasoline delivery truck with his father and his uncle. They were welcoming him in reassurance of his purpose.

Manolo didn't blink an eye as he guided the Lucia straight to a place on the coastline that only a few knew. Suddenly a light appeared on the shore line at the base of the rugged terrain of the Trinidad Mountains. The light flickered once and then twice. Then on the third time, Manolo flashed back with his own flashlight. On the shore line waited a fellow warrior who Manolo trusted with his life, he referred to the man only as Raton, *or* Mouse. As anti-Castro rebels, Raton and Manolo had met in their youth while collaborating with the CIA in providing intelligence and smuggling guns into Cuba while making preparations for the Bay of Pigs Invasion in 1961. This Pablo knew from the meetings in Tampa.

"You must trust this man completely boy" Manolo calmly said. The minute you lose trust in him, you have the freedom to abort the mission. *M'entiendes?*"

"Si Señor, entiendo" "Yes I understand Sir"

Raton was Manolo's contact in Cuba and the person who was to guide Pablo to the location of the attempt. Raton waited patiently at the arranged location by the sea where Pablo would be dropped off and picked up once the mission had been accomplished.

The profile on Raton was that he was a farmer in the outskirts of Trinidad who knew the area like the back of his hand. A humble man of modest means, Raton had devoted his life to the task of overthrowing Castro from power. As an ex-member of a Special Forces group of rebels, Raton had fought against the former Cuban Dictator, Fulgencio Batista, and alongside Fidel in the Sierra Maestra Mountains. After years of loyal service, Raton had defected from Castro's army once he realized Fidel was a Communist. He then joined the anti-Castro rebels in the Escambray Mountains and fearlessly fought against the Communist until he was captured by Castro forces and incarcerated. Charged as an enemy of the state involved in anti-revolutionary terrorist activities, Raton was sentenced to twenty years in prison. It was there that he earned the nickname El Raton for having escaped from a number of prisons through self-made underground tunnels—only to be caught and tortured every time.

Old and in ill health, Fidel later determined that Raton wasn't a threat to the state anymore and eventually released him on strict probation. Although Raton had lost his physical might of earlier years, he had never lost his passion for Cuba's freedom. He knew that to free the country he loved from tyranny; the head of the tyrant had to roll. Having been involved with a number of CIA operations, he didn't trust highly sophisticated plots. In his mind, the simpler the plan—the better! His motto was "*Mientras menos bulto más claridad,*" *or* the lesser the bulk, the greater the clarity.

Raton's attitude reassured Pablo of his likeminded purpose. Manolo had told him there had to be mutual trust if they were to succeed in the attempt. As a survivalist, Raton's greatest asset was that he knew the mountains around Trinidad. He also knew Fidel's woman, Delia Soto Del Valle personally and where she lived. Most importantly, Raton knew her daily schedule.

As the Lucia approached the coast, Pablo solemnly stood upright on the front of the craft in the darkness of the night. His mind filled with wondering thoughts of executing the attack thus fulfilling what he considered to be his life-long purpose. Looking towards the shoreline in the distance, Pablo noticed Raton's tall figure dressed in black, holding a high-power flashlight in his right hand reminiscent of a lighthouse.

As the boat approached the shoreline, Raton walked into the water a few feet, then turned off the light while waving his arms with palms open as to welcome the two. Manolo maneuvered the Lucia slowly closer to shore. In the meantime Pablo slipped his right hand into his pocket and grabbed the rifle bullet squeezing it lightly as to remind himself of his purpose.

"Look around boy," said Manolo while cutting off the engines. "Remember this spot well for it is here that I will pick you up when your mission has been accomplished.

For the time being I will be fishing at Old Viejo Bay looking forward to hearing news of your success."

Pablo nodded in agreement, quickly gathering his backpack then walking to the front of the boat again as to not lose sight of every move the figure on the shoreline was making.

"Do you have your entire belongings boy?"

Upon hearing Manolo's question, Pablo opened the backpack checking the contents for a final time: night vision binoculars; camouflage all weather suit; a compass; climbing rope; one US army fighting knife; one machete and a bag of dried meat. He then placed his hand in the jacket pocket and squeezed the bullet once more.

"Yes Sir, I am all set."

"As long as the M21rifle is in its place, I will take care of business" Pablo concluded turning towards Manolo while looking him in the eye for encouragement. Manolo grinned and winked his left eye with affirmative confidence.

Pablo remained with eyes set on the old man making sure he didn't flinch. He never did. The M21 sniper rifle had been used by the United States Army during the Vietnam War because of its accuracy and the ability for a quick second shot. The weapon had been smuggled into Cuba shortly after Pablo had finished his training in the Everglades; it was now in the hands of a support team member who lived in the mountains near Delia's home.

In his mind Pablo knew of the unavoidable. His sweat covered forehead reflected the anxiety he felt. After ten years in exile, the opportunity to finally silence the voice of the man who he blamed for the death of his father had finally arrived. The time for revenge was near.

Without having to throw anchor, Manolo threw a rope to Raton who pulled the Lucia near enough for Pablo to jump off joining him in the water. After a brief greeting, Raton pushed the Lucia away as Manolo started the engines once again quickly disappearing into the darkness of the night.

"The name is Pablo isn't it?"

"Si Señor!"

"Como estas? How are you?" asked Raton as the two made their way to the shoreline.

"Bien y Usted? Fine and you?"

"Bien Gracias." answered Raton with a look of fulfillment on his face.

"It is pleasure to meet a young man of patriotic principles."

"Thank you Sir, the same goes for you"

Raton smiled ardently looking into Pablo's eyes as to confirm authenticity.

During his training Pablo had been advised to look at men like Raton straight in the eyes. These types of men were bold and honest, and could tell dishonesty in the eyes— Pablo knew of its consequences.

"From this moment on we have each other's back. We are brothers in the cause of freedom. We are now one. *M'entiendes*?" Raton said assertively

"Absolutely Sir, I understand." Pablo responded feeling at ease with Raton.

"Good! I am glad we got that out of the way. Let us go now, morning is approaching."

In seconds, the two had vanished from the area like predators in the night. They crossed a solitary country road and into Raton's corroded 1957 Chevy truck from the pre-Castro days which he had hidden in thick bushes in a field. Without saying a word Raton started up the old truck and put it in gear rapidly separating the two from the spot.

Raton, a wide framed man, defiantly wore a faded N.Y. Yankee cap that protected a clean shaven head. His sharp-featured face with noticeable scars woven deeply within his wrinkles was a testimony of the battle ridden life which had preceded him. His large callused hands held the steering wheel of his old faithful tightly. The file on Raton revealed a good man, a patriot who would gladly accept a straight ticket to hell for the sake of killing the man he had labeled as the bearded bastard.

"Forgive me for asking, but with all due respect, what is your real name Sir? I don't feel comfortable calling you Raton."

"Don't you worry about my name son, I only allow friends to call me Raton." the old warrior said with a confidant smirk on his face.

"Gracias, the feeling is mutual," Pablo responded feeling at peace with Raton's answer.

"By the way Raton, what do you have under the hood of this beast?"

"You know much about trucks son?"

"No, not really but I know a powerful machine when I see it!"

Raton smiled and proceeded to answer with pride in his voice. "You are right boy, this is indeed a powerful truck, it has a modified 408w Chevy Stroker 450HP. Do you know what that means?"

"No sir, not really"

"Well, put it this way, in terms of how fast it can go, imagine us hitting one hundred mph before you can count your age."

Pablo looked at Raton with eyebrows raised.

"Why so much engine Sir"

"You will soon find out." said Raton facetiously, he then pressed the pedal to the metal long enough to let Pablo feel the power of his old Chevy ½ ton pickup, racing west on Highway 12, through the foothills of the Escambray Mountains.

"Just out of curiosity, where did you get such a powerful motor Sir?"

Turning to Pablo once again Raton smiled and while pointing to his cap he said, "America, where the best trucks in the World are made!"

"But how did you…"

"It was smuggled into the country illegally, just like your weapon of choice. You see boy, our people here have learned to survive and live another day, hoping that perhaps someone, somewhere, someday, may be crazy enough to kill the bearded bastard so we can all be free again, like the Americans."

Pablo's demeanor changed suddenly, he then reached into his coat pocket and squeezed the bullet. Pausing briefly he thought of Raton's reference to Castro. It was the same one Ramón had used when he handed him the bullet. Noticing his every move, Raton became concerned about his unexpected facial change.

"Que pasa—what's wrong boy? Did I say something wrong?"

"Oh no Sir, you didn't. I was just scratching my leg."

Pablo didn't speak again for a while, thinking of what Raton had said with regards to the people and their hope. He then realized the greater purpose of the attack; in his hands was the liberation of the Cuban people, the stakes had just gotten higher. When at one time the honoring of his Father and Grandparents memory was his motivation for killing Castro; patriotism now claimed its righteous place in Pablo's heart. The further he traveled inland with Raton, the more committed he became.

Chapter Seven

The Mill

The two traveled in silence for a while on the dark-open road. As they approached the farming town of Gavilan, the familiar sound of roosters crowing in the countryside broke the monotony of their travel. An abandoned sugar mill in the outskirts of town was to be the first stop before daylight. From there they would move to La Sierrita, a mountain side town heavily populated with anti Castro rebels and the location where Pablo was to receive his instruction for the final part of the attack. Raton had blazed through the back roads of the countryside with reckless abandon, knowing the importance of night travel. He then slowed down and with flashlight in hand he looked intently towards the high wire fence beyond the thick brush on the side of the road.

"What is it Sir?"

"Coño—Dammed! If I could only have my eyesight back again I'd do anything. You know boy, at one time I could spot a freckle on a cow's ass. Today, I can barely see the damn cow! I am looking for the opening on the fence."

"Look there it is," said Pablo pointing to a gap in the bushes on the side of the road.

Without hesitation, Raton maneuvered his pickup through the bushes on to a narrow trail, and on through a cut out hole in the heavily spiked wire fence with a Peligro—Danger sign posted on it. Shortly after crossing a narrow creek and in sight of the imposing large sugar mill building in the distance, Raton made a sharp right turn into the overgrown brush, parking the truck behind an abandoned wooden shed.

The old warrior appeared to be in his element. He opened the screechy door of his truck grabbing his machete from underneath the seat. He then walked to a nearby tree swiftly cutting down two large branches from it, placing them over the truck. Confident as if his every move had been well rehearsed, Raton walked ahead of Pablo.

"Come on son, from here on we walk," the old man said grabbing his military duffel bag from the bed of the truck. He then led Pablo out of the brush and on to a grassy dirt road which led to the Mill.

"This is government property isn't it sir?"

"Not really Son." Raton said decisively.

"What do you mean Sir?" Pablo insisted knowing there was more to Raton's comment.

Raton didn't answer right away; he just walked steadily kicking rocks from time to time with his worn-out commando boots. Pablo respected his silence, yet remained interested. Raton then stopped walking near the abandoned mill, took a deep breath and proceeded to answer Pablo's question while staring at the imposing old building.

"What I meant was that this sugar mill was founded by my grandfather at the turn of the century, he named it El Central Azucarero Santa Ana—the Santa Ana Sugar Mill, after his mother." Pausing for a moment while looking at the shell of what had once been the greatest sugar producing mill in the south region of Cuba, he then continued, "All throughout its history it had produced thousands of tons of sugar and employed hundreds of workers who supported their families and their communities." he said with great pride in his voice. "You see boy, back in the 1950s and before Castro nationalized the sugar industry, Cuba milled an average of 43.9 million metric tons of sugarcane at a rate of 507,000 metric tons per day, producing 5.63 million metric tons of sugar per year. Today, Cuba's sugar production ranges from 1 to 1.5 million metric tons per year. That is what happens when the Communist touch anything, they believe government control is the answer, not hard working, well compensated, God fearing men like my Grandfather."

Raton then stopped talking, but this time Pablo wasn't going to let him off the hook, he wanted the complete story. This was yet another reason to kill the bearded bastard.

"Please continue Sir, I need to know more."

Raton slowly turned his head towards the young man looking at him with a piercing look in his eyes which revealed his deep rooted anger that could only be appeased with the success of their planned attack.

Satisfied with Pablo's sincerity, Raton went on. "Shortly after the government took over the sugar operations at the Santa Ana, production diminished until it closed in 1970; after the regime's failed attempt to produce one hundred million tons of sugar nations wide. The regime then used the buildings to temporarily house and torture anti-government political prisoners."

"How do you know about this Sir?"

"I was one of them!"

"What do you mean?"

"I saw it with my own eyes boy. For two months they kept me tied up, interrogating and torturing me at all times of the day and night."

"What happened then Sir?"

"I never said a word. They eventually left me alone without food or water hoping I would die" Raton then let out a thunderous laugh that echoed on the outer walls of the abandoned mill. Unable to restrain himself, Pablo laughed along in celebration of the old man's resilient attitude against all odds. For that one moment their laughter revealed their shared spirit of defiance. Their souls were bonding and they knew it. They also knew the seriousness of their ultimate goal.

After a short break to catch his breath, Raton concluded. "I later escaped through a hole on the roof, doing the same wherever I was incarcerated, thus earning my nick name El Raton." Pablo listened carefully to every word

Raton spoke knowing it was a painful subject to talk about.

Raton then stopped talking, lifting his head towards

the sun rising in the sky to the east of the Mill. He then

proceeded to walk silently with Pablo by his side. Feeling

Raton's energy with every step, Pablo remembered his

parents talking about the Castro's killing fields when he was

a small boy. Raton's words resonated deeply in Pablo's

heart, as he wondered why it was that the world didn't seem

to care about the regime's crimes against humanity.

Nothing more was said as the two cautiously

approached the old mill. Raton's rapid pace slowed down

then he stopped and dropped to one knee. Pablo followed

thinking Raton had detected movement up ahead. Raton

swiftly dropped his military duffel bag to the ground and

opened it in one motion. Pablo remained crotched just below

the thick tall weeds on the side of the dirt road; attentively keeping his eyes on Raton's every move. Raton pulled two 9 mm handguns out of his bag, he looked at Pablo signaling him to remain quiet then handed him one of the guns with a silencer attached.

Pablo didn't know what to make of the unexpected situation, so he followed orders. Following Raton's hand motions, Pablo went into the high grass moving south and towards the imposing structure at the end while keeping a close eye on Raton who approached the old mill on the left. Once they had made it within a few feet of a large opening that was once the sugar cane unloading station door, Raton moved ahead with weapon raised, hugging the bullet ridden wall with feather-light movement, disappearing into the interior blackness.

Uncertain of the situation, Pablo quickly moved aggressively towards the building, also going inside through a window space on the other side from where Raton had entered. With cat like instincts and weapon in hand, Pablo hit the ground immediately ready to attack. Remaining still on the dust filled floor, he assessed the surroundings hoping to see Raton, but he had vanished in seconds. Could it be a trap, Pablo wondered or was it a sick trick played by the old warrior to test his readiness.

Lifting himself off the floor and knowing the potential danger, Pablo placed his pistol in the back of his pants and pulled out his fighting knife from the side of his boot. He proceeded to walk in the direction of the opening through which Raton had entered the building. Hugging the wall with knife firmly held in attack mode, Pablo noticed a crouched shadow of a man hiding behind a large stack of tires near the entryway. Unable to get a good read on the person's identity, Pablo zeroed in on his target reaching it in a matter of seconds. It was Raton.

Raton clearly appeared to be ready for a surprise attack on whoever walked through the door. Perhaps he had thought Pablo would follow him through the large opening.

What he didn't know was that Pablo's survival instincts had led him through a different entrance to the building. Without hesitation Pablo quietly snuck up on him from behind, grabbed a handful of his hair, and pulling it back he firmly placed the razor sharp knife on his neck.

"If you so much as blink your eyes, I'll kill you!" Pablo whispered in his ear while removing Raton's gun from his hand. Pablo then continued to whisper in Raton's ear.

"I don't know what your game is old man? But I came here with the single purpose of killing only one man. Please understand that if there are other casualties along the way, I will not lose sleep over it."

Knowing the seriousness of the moment Raton then smiled and said, "Relax boy, you have passed the first test!"

Cautiously trusting in Raton's words, Pablo slowly removed the knife from his throat. Raton then turned around facing his young accomplice looking him in the eye with a greater level of respect. He extended his right hand and waited for Pablo to return the friendly gesture. After a moment of thought Pablo reached out knowing he had made his point clear.

The two shook hands firmly and embraced knowing where each stood. Raton then reached out and ruffled the young man's hair; "You remind me of myself thirty years ago" he said and walked away towards the back of the building.

"Come on boy; let's find a place to rest."

Pablo followed Raton towards a hidden corner of the warehouse, looking around the deserted mill, amazed at its mammoth size, and wondering what it must have been like in its glory days. Noticing a slither of daylight creeping through a crack on a side wall big enough for him to look through, Pablo walked slowly towards it as Raton quietly observed the young man's interest. Pablo was very fond of his country's history as well as its mornings; it reminded him of his childhood home a few miles away from where he now stood.

Hugging the wall once again as to not be visible from the outside, he peeked through the crack and stood still looking through it. The sun was rising in the distant east of the land he loved. There he stood, nose pressed on the cool concrete wall savoring the sweet smell of earth that was his own, with eyes fixed on the green horizon beyond and sun creeping above the royal palms, Pablo knew he was back home. It had been a long time since he had experience the sunrise of his beloved Cuba. There he stood for a while under the watchful eye of the old warrior whose mind also drifted to a place and time that would never be again, unless…!

Pablo remembered the days when he was young and his father would take him to the countryside on his old truck to deliver gasoline to the farmers around his hometown of Cienfuegos. It was there when he first fell in love with El Campo *or* the countryside. Pablo remembered much more than the common person, he remembered his childhood friends and Olga his first love. He remembered days when his Mother laughed and sang love songs while hanging fresh laundry in the back-yard lines of their home. He especially remembered the smell of his Abuela's freshly baked pumpernickel bread and his pet rooster, *Pichilingo*.

Perhaps it was his inability to let go of those days that brought him back. In his heart Pablo wanted his life back, even though he knew things had changed. He just hoped God would also understand what he was about to do.

After a while, he turned towards Raton who waited patiently in a dark corner of the mill.

"Come and have a seat son," the old man said with a calm voice. "We will be spending the day here and move out again when the sun goes down."

Pablo complied, knowing he needed to rest for the next part of the journey which was to take him back to Cienfuegos, his hometown to visit his Grandparent's grave.

Once there, he would stay at his childhood friend Rolando's home until word came from the mountains to proceed with the mission. Finding space on the floor a few feet from Raton, Pablo placed his backpack against the wall, laying his head on it. Relaxed and confidant in their new level of mutual understanding, Pablo slept and dreamed of thundering storms. Unable to sleep, Raton watched over Pablo wondering if his new associate would have the courage to finish the job.

Chapter Eight

Cienfuegos

The midday Cuban sun suspended in the cloudless Cuban sky was scorching everything beneath it, especially the tin roof in the back of the mill where the two attempted to rest before engaging in their night travels. Thirsty and drenched in his own sweat, Pablo drank from his canteen then walked to the crack on the wall looking through it once again as if he expected to find something different. Looking toward the highway, he saw an olive green military truck traveling east on the Highway 12.

"I take it these scumbags have a military post nearby, huh?"

"What do you mean son?"

"I just saw one of their vehicles pass by on the highway."

"No there isn't any post around here. The whole country has become a military post. That's how they rule the people—intimidation."

"Things haven't changed much, have they?" Pablo responded in disgust.

"No they haven't. As a matter of fact, persecution has gotten worse lately. Ever since those kids busted through the Peruvian embassy in Havana, the country is on full alert. They tell us that the imperialist Yankees are behind the Peruvian Embassy issues in Havana. And that we should prepare for a Yankee invasion from the north. The truck you saw today is a good thing."

"What do you mean sir?"

"That military truck is evidence that our intelligence is accurate."

"I don't understand."

"Allow me to explain," said Raton while walking toward Pablo at the wall. Placing his hand over Pablo's shoulder he calmly said, "That truck you saw earlier was headed for the city of Trinidad, this is further evidence that the government is enhancing security around Dalia's home in preparation for the bastard's visit. *M'entiendes?"*

Pablo listened attentively to every word Raton spoke knowing his team had been carefully surveying the area in preparation for an attack.

"There is something you need to know son," Raton continued, "that Bearded Bastard, who the world considers the Robin Hood of the Americas is nothing less than a coward."

"What do you mean?" Pablo questioned hoping to instigate the old warrior into the emotional outrage he was known for.

"You want to know, well let me tell you." Raton noticing the shadows of sunset gathered his belongings from the warehouse in preparation for the night travel.

"That bastard has always been a yellow belly! We know that as a young leader at the University of Havana, he talked a good game, but when it came down to throwing it down, he had others do the fighting for him, just like a coward. A COWARD, that's what he is!" Raton screamed from the top of his lungs and stormed out of the mill.

Pablo unable to restrain himself any longer busted out laughing as he followed Raton on to the dirt road and back to the truck, having succeeded in getting him upset.

"Raton, wait! You didn't finish the story."

Raton stopped abruptly. "What story? " He asked disturbed.

"The one about the truck!"

Raton didn't answer for a moment, he then kicked the dirt and with a grin on his face he shouted to the wind, "Son of a ...! You got me didn't you? Manolo told you to tick-me-off so you could see one of my rampaging fits didn't he. Son of a b...?"

The two then laughed uncontrollably for a moment. Realizing the possible danger of being detected by the military they stopped.

"Well, it's something like that." Pablo responded." "But I am serious Sir; please finish telling me the story?"

"Well, as I was saying, Fidel always let others do the fighting for him while he escaped like a rat. Now that all hell is breaking loose in Havana, he is running again—this time into our trap."

Pablo knew exactly what he meant, El Comandante—The Commander and Chief was expected in Trinidad soon and the truck was evidence of the security buildup in the region.

By the time night had completely fallen, the two were well on their way to Cienfuegos where Pablo's friend Rolando waited for him at his farm outside of town. Rolando had decided to support the operation from the minute he found out about it through Raton. His home was on two acres of property that his grandmother Fina had left him when she died. The government had originally confiscated the land, but later granted it back to him with the condition that he raised chickens for the state. Ever since their childhood days, he and Pablo had been close. Once Rolando was approached to be a part of the attempt, he offered his home for Pablo to stay at while he remained in Cienfuegos.

In the early days of the revolution, when the Communists took inventory of non-party member's positions, many buried their money and jewelry in the ground. Some built secret compartments in the walls of their home; Fina chose to add an attic space to her home so she could hide her lifelong savings. The attic was well secured and big enough for one person to sleep comfortably. Although there wasn't any money left anymore, the space above the kitchen of the old farm house remained intact.

Rolando was the only person his Grandmother ever told about the attic. This was to become Pablo's safe place until the time came to head to the mountains of Trinidad for the final part of the operation. Rolando's hatred for Castro was equal to Pablo's. He blamed his Grandmother's death on the government takeover of the farm; she became depressed, ultimately dying a short time later. Ever since Castro's take over, Rolando had wanted to leave the country and go to America, but he never had a chance, he was of military age and his visa had been denied on various occasions. This was his opportunity to avenge his Grandmothers death as well as his lost youth.

Forty-five minutes later, Raton and Pablo entered the city of Cienfuegos. This was the one place Pablo held dear in his heart, the place where he was born and where his grandparent's remains rested. The familiarity of his beloved hometown connected him to painful memories he had chosen to forget. Although dark, he could still remember the buildings and the *Flamboyán flower* trees, which once upon a time, served as a landmark for his father while on the gasoline distribution runs.

Not much had changed in the ten years he had been gone, other than the erosion of the roads and the once beautifully maintained buildings were no longer so.

Raton felt comfortable with Rolando's involvement in the plan. In an earlier meeting, Raton had put him through a series of psychological analysis—concluding in approval. In Raton's eyes, Rolando would be a good associate because of his inability to speak as well as his anger against Fidel.

The two drove through the outskirts of the city hoping to avoid being noticed by authorities. Raton knew government forces were lazy and they liked to sleep at night. On their way to Rolando's countryside home, in an area known to the locals as *El Junco,* they passed by the old sleepy cemetery where his Abuelo's remains rested.

With open fields to each side of the road, the moonless night swallowed the presence of any human existence. Having turned off his headlights, Raton slowed down to snail pace traveling east on El Junco road. He then noticed a flickering light in the distance; he turned the trucks lights on and off hoping to promote a response—it was Rolando. Pablo was on edge, although he trusted Raton, he knew this was enemy territory and anything could happen at any time.

The light in the distance flashed twice then moved away from the main road towards a small home at the end of a dirt trail. Raton followed the light slowly surveying the area for any suspicious movement in the dark. The old warrior had a sixth sense about him, sometimes he says he hears voices that speak in his head, but they are mostly good voices. It's the bad voices he worries about, the ones that tell him when he is being betrayed. So far he had not heard those voices at Rolando's farm, so he continued driving, following the figure of a big man who walked on a dirt road with only the stars to guide his path.

Upon arrival, the large person walked towards the driver's side of the truck, Raton stepped outside to greet him, and they then walked towards the passenger side. Realizing the dark large figure was Rolando; Pablo quickly opened the door in anticipation of the long awaited reunion.

"Rolando, is that you?"

Rolando did not speak; he just moved his head in affirmation, and then jumped on his old friend with a long heartfelt embrace. In the silence of the night, only the sobbing of tears could be heard. Raton stood back touched by the moment, and then spoke.

"Pablo, Rolando would like for you to know that he cannot speak."

"What do you mean?" Pablo asked surprised while still holding on to his old friend.

"Rolando lost his voice as the result of a lightning strike that almost killed him shortly after you left. He flat-lined a couple of times on his way to the hospital, the doctors were able to save his life but not his voice. When they went to perform the tracheotomy so he could breathe, they cut his vocal cords. He wanted me to tell you not to worry, that he's okay—happy to be alive."

"But how does he communicate?" Pablo asked upset.

"Don't worry, he says, he first tries doing hand language, if people can't understand him, he then will write on the notepad which he carries with him at all times. If they can't understand
him still, he has a pair of size 12 steel metal boots which can be very persuasive in getting his point across."

Immediately Rolando let out a deep gut sounding laugh shaking the ground underneath. He then grabbed Pablo around the shoulders and led him to the house while Raton drove the truck behind the chicken coop and gathered Pablo's belongings.

For the next two hours, Pablo and Rolando reminisced about their childhood days and how things had changed in their hometown. Raton stood by waiting for a while before he headed back to the hills of Trinidad to connect the final pieces of the puzzle for the bastard's welcoming party.

"Hardly anyone is left in our barrio anymore," Rolando wrote on his pad. "People have either died, left the country for the United States or moved to Havana in search of a better future. Only a few of us remain."

"Anyone I know?"

"Well yes, your childhood sweetheart still lives in town." Rolando wrote.

"Which one?" Pablo asked with a smirk on his face."

"Come on boy! You know which one had stolen your heart, "Rolando wrote then threw the pad at him.

Pablo smiled lowering his head feeling relaxed for the first time since he left Key West.

"Its Olga isn't it?" Pablo asked while looking straight into Rolando's eyes in anticipation of his affirmative answer while handing him the pad.

Rolando dropped the pencil and smiled.

He then wrote again. "Olga married a high ranking government official and became a member of the Communist party herself."

Pablo didn't respond, all he could do was imagine how much Olga had changed and how she would react if she saw him.

"How does she look Rolando?"

"Beautiful as always, like a china doll."

"Do you think we'll have a chance to see her sometime while I am here?"

Rolando's smile went away fast, he then placed the pencil on his old wooden table and looking firmly into

Pablo's eyes he shook his head in obvious disgust. He picked up the pencil and wrote again. "Are you stupid? What if she decides to squeal on you? No, the answer is absolutely not! You are here on a very important assignment; once your mission is accomplished and Cuba is free, you will be able to see her as much as you want. For now we stay focused on the job at hand, not girls!"

"Oh by the way now that you mention girls, is there one in your life?" Pablo asked sarcastically hoping to dig at Rolando.

"No, and even if there was, I wouldn't be thinking about her now."

"Are you sure there isn't someone on the other side of town who has tickled your interest?"

No! Well...no! No one wants a mute with a bad temper anyway, now get your stuff, I am going to show you your quarters," he wrote. Rolando stood up from the table and walked towards the kitchen.

"Rolando wait, what if we happen to run into her in the streets? What then?"

Rolando didn't respond, he just shook his head. For a moment it was like old times when the two were kids and could trigger each other's anger in a split second.

"Okay, okay! I will not pursue Olga but if she finds out about me, I will blame it on you!" Pablo continued bugging Rolando on the matter.

Realizing what was taking place; Rolando stopped, pulled out his pad and pencil and wrote. "Keep it up! You will soon have to speak with a writing pad too!"

"Why does that mean?" Pablo asked sarcastically.

"It means I am going to cut off your lengua, *or* tongue!" Rolando wrote with fire in his eyes, standing only inches from

Pablo with a stern look upon his face. In the other room, Raton stood up from his chair not knowing what to expect. Pablo and Rolando remained still, looking at each other in the eyes. Then the two suddenly burst out in uncontrollable laughter that took them to the floor. Raton finally breathed, relived as he watched the two friends hug each other knowing their bond was solid.

In two short hours, the two old friends had rekindled their friendship. Fulfilled with the first part of the mission, Raton left after a short while knowing that he would soon return for Pablo, and then they would travel back to the Trinidad Mountains.

After Raton's departure, Pablo and Rolando remained silent for a while; only the look in their eyes spoke of their commitment to settle the score with the one they blamed for their country's demise. Both wanted justice for their departed loved ones as well as for those who remained, and those who were still to come.

Meanwhile, Pablo was to stay with Rolando, living in his attic until further word came from Raton. Although concerned for his safety, Raton granted Pablo's request to visit the barrio where he was born and to the cemetery to visit his Abuelo's gravesite for what could be a final farewell.

Chapter Nine

The Cemetery

The night was quiet and serene, yet Pablo's thoughts didn't allow him to sleep, and when he did, he dreamed of turbulent skies and turbulent things he couldn't control. Voices sounded off from all corners of his troubled mind clamoring to be heard, and tortured him until the early hours of the morning when he heard the familiar sound of roosters coming from the back of the house.

'Damn you roosters!' he thought, he then remembered where he was. He looked around the empty attic wondering why it had come to this. He wondered why God had chosen him for this unenviable task—or had He? Why leave the comforts of America and the warmth of loved ones to come to a place where you don't belong anymore? The voice in his head said.

Then in the depth of his thoughts he remembered his childhood and the old black man he had befriended on the steps of the Jagua Theater, at the corner of his street. Demetrio was his name; most times he sat alone until Pablo came to talk to him and listen to his patriot stories. Lonely and forgotten by his own

people, Demetrio had been a decorated soldier during Cuba's war for independence from the Spanish empire.

"Ninety-two I am boy!" He proudly proclaimed. "My eyes have seen much in my days."

"You are a young lad with much to learn," he'd say to Pablo. Then he'd speak of his glory days of youth, his battles and his horse Candela *or* Fire.

"Why did you name her Candela?"

Demetrio always smiled when Pablo showed interest, perhaps he was the only one who cared about the old warrior anymore.

"We fought the Spanish with machetes and on our horses. Sometimes they would set fire to the fields to spook our horses, so they would toss us to the ground. Candela never tossed me, on the contrary she ran through the fire— never fearing."

"Word in the battlefields was that the Spaniards feared Candela and the crazy demon-possessed Negro on her back who they say had many lives. I didn't have many lives, I had faith."

Demetrio had told Pablo that story one hundred times before, and one hundred times Pablo listened to every word. Demetrio was a good man, not a Negro as the racist Spaniards like to call him—he was a patriot and his friend. Perhaps it was Demetrio's stories that made Pablo feel patriotically responsible.

"Patria y Dios *or* Country and God!" the gentle old man would often say. "Everything else is fleeting boy—like the wind."

Demetrio had taught Pablo great values on those lazy summer days on San Carlos Street.

"You will suffer much son!" he'd say. "Not because you want to, but because you care. *For he who loves deeply, hurts deeply.* I never thought it would come to this boy, we fought for

freedom—not this!" He'd say about Communism with tears in his tired eyes.

In the loneliness of his own space, Pablo understood what the old man meant. In his mind he was destined to do what needed to be done, and nothing was going to change that.

Pablo's silent thoughts were interrupted by two knocks on the attic floor door; Rolando was signaling the night was upon them and the coast was clear. Three knocks meant it wasn't. This was the protocol to follow during the time Pablo would remain hidden at Rolando's home. The windows and lights remained on as always, so as to not look suspicious. Pablo would remain, limited to using only the kitchen and a bathroom in the back of the house.

The first day passed without incident, as the two friends continued to share stories of their growing up days in the streets of their old barrio. They also shared personal matters that brought back painful memories of the last ten years since Pablo had been gone. Much had happened in their lives as well as in the place they once called home.

Communism had brought with it much pain and sorrow. The government control and the day-to-day struggle to survive had consumed people's existence. Like animals in the wild, finding food had become their main objective. In line with the Communist manifesto, government had taken the place of God in Cuba. The Caesar philosophy of divide and conquer had been systematically implemented into society through moral decay and intimidation. Neighborhood government spying had become the norm.

People didn't trust each other anymore, leaving little hope for developing an opposition front.

Fully aware of the limited time they had to be together, the two focused on their mission to visit the town's cemetery that night.

"What do you use for transportation these days Rolando?" Pablo asked, not having seen a vehicle on the property.

Once night had completely fallen, Rolando smiled and signaled for Pablo to follow him in the direction of a neglected barn in the back of his property. He carefully opened the large wooden doors revealing his prized possession. There sat a 1967 Volkswagen Beatle.

"That is your father's old car isn't it Rolando?"

Rolando smiled proudly and proceeded to pull out his writing pad from his back pocket.

"That is the same bug that took us on that trip to the countryside on the same day your family received the telegram of freedom—remember?"

"Yep—it sure is!" Pablo joyfully replied.

"My father left it for me; I repaired it making sure to silence the muffler for this mission." Rolando then reached inside and pulled out a small bag and handed it to Pablo and signaled for him to open it.

"What is it?" Pablo asked, and then proceeded to open the bag pulling out a fake beard.

"What's this, some kind of a joke?"

Rolando shook his head and laughed. "No joke" he wrote. "That's for you to wear tonight when we go into town, the last thing we need is for someone to recognize you. It was my father's; I believe he wore it to disguise himself when he was on sales trips out of town"

"Why would he wear such a thing?" Pablo asked baffled.

"I don't know maybe he wasn't supposed to be in those places. Maybe he had some other business I don't care to find out about. Whatever the case is, the beard is now yours—wear it!" Pablo didn't object knowing Rolando was right. Their time together had been pleasant, but they both understood the seriousness of their arrangement. Going back into their old barrio was a favor Raton had granted Pablo at his request. This was to be *un entra y sale*—an in and out visit, taking no more than a couple of hours. They would then return to Rolando's home and wait for word from the mountains.

Shortly before 11:00 P.M, Rolando rolled the Bug out of the barn, and with lights off, he pulled it next to the house in pitch blackness. Pablo quickly jumped into the back seat and underneath empty boxes Rolando had previously arranged in case of a government roadblock. He then drove out of his property slowly, turning west on the Junco Road and towards the city of Cienfuegos a few minutes away.

The short drive served Pablo well, as his mind traveled back in time when he and Rolando walked through El Junco, eating mangos and chasing butterflies and dreams. But they were different now. They had both been scarred by the battles of life and he knew they could never go back to the days they once knew. Darkness had descended solemnly upon the countryside of Cuba's southern region. Much had been written about that area in history books. This was the motherland of the Guajiro *or* the farmer, who for centuries had lived off the land with great pride, always understanding integrity and patriotism. Pablo knew this because his father Felo was one!

The glow of distant dim lights revealed their proximity to that place Pablo held close to his heart. Cienfuegos had been and would always remain his true love. The two friends had glanced at each other periodically—they both understood the risk involved. They knew that the long and laborious planning of the assassination attempt could go up in smoke in a matter of seconds if caught by government officials. As potentially dangerous as it was, this visit to Cienfuegos validated Pablo's reason for returning, and in his heart Rolando knew it.

Sitting up, Pablo noticed the first welcoming sign to his beloved city. The long road of royal palms still stood tall and glorious on the corner of Junco Road and Manacas Street. There Rolando turned right towards the barrio of Glorytown, the cradle of their youth. Knowing of the potential danger of being seen, Pablo's back stiffened with tension and his palms began to sweat as did the back of his neck. The overflowing adrenalin could only compare to that which he felt in Key West when he met Manolo on that gloomy foggy morning on the boat dock. Ten years had passed since he said goodbye to Glorytown, never thinking he'd return as long as the Castro regime remained in power.

To be caught by the authorities now would mean certain death by firing squad—they both knew that.

As destiny would have it, Pablo was back. Unfortunately, no welcoming committee or street parade awaited him for having made it to the major leagues like he had often dreamed when he was young. This time he had returned as a stranger in the shadows of the night.

Like a dream, he now floated back to his hometown, periodically noticing the fleeting signs of Fidel on the side of the road proclaiming victory over the imperialist Yankees. Pablo wondered why God had allowed this whole mess to happen. Why Fidel, why this beautiful place? He thought. What a fool he thought of Castro, sickened by the sight. If only he knew how irrelevant he was about to become.

As the two rolled into the old city on their way to San Carlos Street and at exactly 11:00 P.M, the town lights went out.

"¡*Apagon*!" Pablo exclaimed.

Rolando nodded shrugging his shoulders as if to say, 'same old crap.' This was Rolando's plan all along; he knew the lights went off at exactly 11:00 P.M. every night. Most nights the lights would stay off all night, giving them greater freedom to move around the city without being noticed and eventually make their way to the cemetery. But first Rolando wanted Pablo to see the tree covered boulevard of El Prado. This is the place where for generations the young and old went to see and be seen. Unfortunately, the boulevard had lost its luster as it had become a meeting place for young prostitutes better known to the locals as *Jineteras*.

The two strolled slowly down memory lane in the shadows of the night, along the way noticing a few lonely souls still out walking the main boulevard with the hope of finding action from the Soviet sailors who often frequented *El Prado* from the nearby seaport. Rolando wrote.

Upon seeing the action, Pablo became enraged at how young many of the girls appeared to be. Dressed cheaply and all made up, the girls walked with flashlights showing off their stuff hoping to make a deal with those who loved the night. Most of them appeared to be underage girls, who had resorted to prostitution for the sake of providing for their desperate families. Pablo shook his head as Rolando stared at him with frustration in his eyes, his sister had become one of them, Pablo later found out.

Once off the boulevard and on San Carlos Street, they headed north towards their old barrio. Rolando wanted to show Pablo his Grandparents home as well as the *Jagua* Theater and their elementary school. Pablo didn't say much, he just looked around in disbelief. In only ten years, the neighborhood looked gloomy and sad. Even in the darkness of the night, the destruction of the once beautiful city was unmistakable. From what Pablo could tell, many of the buildings desperately needed paint and repair. Pablo's frustrations intensified, reaffirming the purpose of his return.

Upon arrival on the block in which they had both been born, Rolando slowed down. Pablo silently broke down in tears as they passed by his Grandparents home. Rolando touched by his friend's emotions, also sobbed quietly while he drove past their street turning south on Manacas Street and on to the Tomas Acea Cemetery a few miles away.

Things had changed on San Carlos Street, but that didn't matter, the old barrio had been, and would forever remain the cradle of Pablo's youth. Although Pablo was now a proud American citizen, his heart yearned to see his birthplace free. For him this was not a matter of citizenship; it was a matter of honor.

After a long drive through the dark streets of Cienfuegos, the tall concrete walls of the cemetery appeared on the right side of the lonely road. As they approached the steel rod gate at the entrance, Rolando noticed a security guard walking in the direction of the car from behind the gate. Rolando slowly motioned for Pablo to scoot down on the seat and pretend to be asleep as they had planned earlier. The guard approached the car with flashlight in one hand and weapon in the other. Peeking from underneath his cap, Pablo who pretended to be asleep, also reached for his weapon, keeping his finger loosely on the trigger of his 9mm, while Rolando pulled out his pad and pencil.

"Buenas noches compañero" "Good evening comrade! How can I help you?" The stern-face young officer asked with weapon in hand.

Rolando pointed to his throat motioning to the now suspicious officer that he had no voice. He then wrote on the pad, "I am a mute and this is my brother from out of town, he's sleeping. We just drove in from Havana and he wanted to visit our Grandparents tomb before heading to my home in the country a few miles away.

"Wake him up, I want to see his face," the officer requested firmly.

Rolando tapped Pablo gently hoping not to rattle him knowing where his right hand was. Pablo removed the cap from his face and rubbed his eyes pretending to be exhausted.

"*Que pasa hermano*?" or "What's going on brother?"

Without hesitation Rolando signaled towards the officer looking at Pablo with wide eyes as if to say, relax.

"Yes Sir, Officer, what seems to be the problem?"

"There is no problem, and there isn't going to be one right?" The officer suggested.

"No Sir, not at all. We were just hoping to visit our Grandparents tomb tonight so we don't have to come all the way back tomorrow." Pablo pleaded.

"You understand what time it is right?" The officer asked sarcastically. "You do understand the country is on high alert—right!"

"No Sir, we didn't know" Pablo replied. "What's going on?"

"The Yankees have started problems again at the Peruvian Embassy in Havana. You should know that!"

"No sir we didn't, I am sorry." Pablo answered while keeping his hand on his weapon.

Concerned about a possible confrontation, Rolando reached in his pocket while signaling for the officer to wait. He pulled twenty pesos out of his pocket and handed it to him hoping he wouldn't get upset. The officer didn't respond he just stood there looking at the two with serious reservations. He then reached out for the money, grabbed it and walked away.

Not knowing what he would do, Rolando waited, Pablo unstrapped his 9 mm holding it between his legs. The officer then slowly walked to the gate and opened it. As the car was about to pass through it, the guard stopped them once again looking at Pablo suspiciously then said,   "You have twenty minutes, don't make me go get you."

"Yes Sir," Pablo responded with fire in his eyes. This was the same arrogant behavior he remembers when he had been abused by Communist teachers and officers when he was a child. For a second he thought of blasting the Communist bastard, but he restrained himself knowing of the greater purpose for which he had returned.

Rolando then drove straight to the tomb; he had been a pallbearer for both of his grandparents. Pablo stepped out of the car cautiously looking back in the direction of the guard at the front of the cemetery. He then moved toward the tomb overwhelmed with emotion. Rolando seeing his friend's painful sorrow placed his arm over him and stood nearby in vigilant silence, neither of them trusting the guard.

Much went through Pablo's mind at that moment as he stood in front of their modest headstone in the ground, with the names, Ana and Julian, engraved underneath two love birds. Pablo then thought of his Abuelo's words of wisdom when as a child he would speak of killing Fidel whenever he saw his Mama cry. Abuelo Julian would say, *"If you kill Fidel, you will be a killer like he is—that is not pleasing to God."*

Although Pablo knew it was wise council, those were words Pablo didn't want to hear, even as a child. He had left the country when his Abuelo's were alive and well, but now they were dead and gone. Pain stricken and distraught, the only thing that brought him peace was the thought of killing the one person who he long ago had judged and convicted as guilty of his pain. A few minutes later they silently walked away from the gravesite to the car.

Chapter Ten

The Call

In the blackness of the night, the two drove from the cemetery knowing the second most important part of the mission had been accomplished; now the rest remained. The disturbing thought of not seeing his Abuelo's alive was behind him now, visiting their graveside had cleansed him of some pain, yet he wondered why Rolando cared so much.

"Why do you have to be so accommodating Rolando? You don't owe me anything man." Pablo suddenly expressed in frustration. "Why do you give a damn?"

Rolando turned looking at Pablo as if he had stepped on his toe, then gave him the middle finger. Pablo immediately broke out in laughter, angering Rolando even more. Unable to control himself, Pablo reached over and grabbed Rolando's head, then kissed him on his forehead knowing what he meant. Rolando pushed Pablo's face away in disgust, and then smiled.

Heading back to town the two remained silent knowing their bond was as strong now as when they were growing up on San Carlos Street.

Rolando had never changed. He was as committed to freedom now, as when he was young. The streets of their hometown were dark and lonely because of the *apagónones* or lights-out. He remembered the places they passed along the way yet he didn't comment on it, for he knew that without the Bastard, soon things would be back to what they used to be. These were the streets the two had walked often, when chasing girls and butterflies mattered most. Perhaps it was Pablo's reluctance to let go of those childhood days that brought him back. In his mind, it was also the reason Raton, Manolo and Ramón fought for freedom of their land. Many were the mitigating thoughts in Pablo's mind as to justify shedding another man's blood. Nonetheless, the Bearded

Bastard was guilty of genocide against his own people and for the violation of his childhood, he deserved to die.

Upon reaching San Carlos Street, Rolando didn't turn left to head back to his place as he should have. Instead he drove on then turned right towards the barrio of Tulipan.

"What are you doing boy?" Pablo asked surprised.

Rolando just smiled and drove on.

"You can smile like an idiot all you want, but I need to know where you are going." Pablo asked seriously.

"Relax *Don Juan!*" Rolando wrote on his pad while driving and grinning.

It was now 1:00 A. M and Pablo remained cautiously attentive, knowing the dangers that surrounded him. Every second he remained in enemy territory and outside of the well strategized arrangement presented a threat to the mission. The slightest slip in the plans could jeopardize the whole operation. Although Fidel was not expected to travel to Trinidad for a couple of days, the orders were to remain at Rolando's place until Raton called with orders.

"Why Tulipan, Rolando?" Pablo asked again.

Rolando only answered with a hand signal to wait as he continued to drive up Santa Cruz Ave past the projects and beyond the mango curve where the two had spent much time together eating mangos from the giant trees.

As they approached the second curve on the winding road, Rolando pulled over to the side and into a bush-filled trail bordering an open field. On the other side stood a large home which Pablo recognized from his early days when he visited with his father and where he saw the beautiful girl for the first time. Barely able to see because of darkness, Pablo suddenly realized what Rolando was doing; he had taken him to the home where Olga lived when they were young. "You son of a...good mother. I can't believe you!"

Rolando let out a heart-felt sound of irrepressible laughter, and then clapped his hands passionately revealing his adolescent side. Pablo seeing signs of his friend's childlike ways couldn't help but to laugh with him. Ten years had passed since Pablo had left the country, but at that moment not a day had gone by. They had sworn to be forever friends when they were young and neither had forgotten their childhood pact.

"So what's the deal boy?"

Rolando laughed again, this time pulling a small flashlight out of his pocket, put it in his mouth and wrote on the pad again.

"Listen, why don't we catch a nap here and in the morning we will head back home after you've seen Olga— this may be your only chance to see her."

"What do you mean?"

"Well, from what I have been told, Olga and her husband moved in with her mother after her father died." Rolando continued to write.

"She's married? Why would I want to interfere with her marriage?"

"I didn't mean for you to interfere with her marriage, idiot. I only meant for you to see her!" Rolando wrote.

Pablo didn't respond knowing in his heart, he would love to see her. He also knew the potential danger of them getting caught by the authorities who would love to proclaim yet another victory over the imperialist Yankees.

"Nah, we better not stay, I am concerned about being out here in the daylight." Pablo reluctantly replied.

Not willing to give up so easy, Rolando insisted. "We only have three hours before the roosters start crowing." he wrote and smiled.

"From the look of things, it appears as if you have greater interest in seeing her than I do." replied the smirking Pablo.

"Now tell me, what would she want with a mute? Look Pablo, Raton told me it would be a couple of days before we were to head to the mountains anyway. Why don't we catch a short nap and I promise you we will head back in the early morning."

Pablo once again took a moment to think about his friend's persistency. Then looking him in the eye as if to see his reaction he said, "Ok we'll stay but if something happens, I will personally break your right hand! You understand?"

Rolando smiled knowing there was no real danger in staying, or in Pablo's threat. He also knew more about Olga than he let Pablo know. Ever since he had been contacted by Raton to be a part of the plot and knowing that Pablo would be staying with him for a couple of days, Rolando had traveled to Tulipan on various occasions to spy on Olga. He knew that she took the 6:00A.M bus to school where she taught second grade.

By 5:30 Rolando was up at the sound of the first rooster's crow, he awakened Pablo who startled reached for his weapon. Rolando appeased him by pointing to his watch, then signaled to his eyes as if to say look, she will soon be catching the bus.

Pablo rubbed his tired eyes yawning; he then heard a door shut in the distance. Upon seeing the figure of a woman, Rolando hit his arm lightly and pointed towards the home in the distance. Pablo looked and stopped breathing for a moment pulling out his small binoculars from the side pocket of his jacket—it was Olga. Rolando remained still while Pablo indulged himself in the beauty that had once been the love of his childhood.

Olga walked to the bus stop and sat on the bench by the side of the road. Rolando started up the bug and began to drive out of the bushes. Pablo immediately reacted by grabbing Rolando by his arm thinking he'd lost it.

"What are you doing?" he asked firmly.

Rolando stooped the car and wrote again. "Relax man! I am going to say hello to her."

"What! Have you lost it—are you crazy?"

"No I am not crazy" he wrote with a smile on his face. "Fix your beard, it's crooked!"

Pablo, trusting Rolando knew what he was doing, straightened the mustache and pulled his cap down to where his eyes were barely visible. Olga, in the distance stood distinguished, even while sitting on the wooden bench at the bus stop. Unassuming, she read from a newspaper looking up occasionally. The light blue Bug approached slowly grabbing her attention; she briefly looked up then went back to her reading not recognizing the occupants in the car. Rolando parked on the side of the road and walked in her direction with a friendly smile on his face. Olga then recognized him and exploded with joyful emotion hugging Rolando for a moment. The two had been good friends when they were young and although many years had passed she had not forgotten him.

Pablo remained in the car admiring her unchanged beauty. Her hair short and black, her big brown eyes glittering with joy radiated like the morning sun. Olga had not changed much over the years. In Pablo's eyes she remained the beauty queen he had fallen in love with when they were both innocent and young. After a few minutes and after having achieved his goal, Rolando said goodbye to her and walked back to the car. He then proceeded to drive away slowly as Pablo's and Olga's eyes connected, then faded away.

"What was that all about?" Pablo asked.

Rolando shrugged his shoulders and ginned not responding.

"She's aged well hasn't she?"

Rolando raising his eye brows nodded in agreement.

"Dammed Rolando, I wish you could talk"

Rolando just smiled and shrugged his shoulders proclaiming ignorance—then drove back home before the sun surfaced and military activity intensified.

🐟 🐟 🐟

Visiting the cemetery had been healing for Pablo, who for too long had fought the tears of his broken heart. Seeing Olga had brought back pleasant memories of brighter days gone by, yet his purpose remained one that required his complete and undivided attention.

The trip back to Rolando's place went smooth. All along, Pablo thought of Olga and of how odd it was to be back inside the lion's den after his parents had sacrificed so much to save him from the misery of living there.

Upon arrival, Rolando drove straight into the barn. The two swiftly made their way back to the house with Pablo retiring to his quarters in the attic shortly after. The day passed without incident as they waited for word from Raton. By sundown, Pablo was about to explode with restless energy. Waiting around in hiding was worse than death, so he decided to make his way down to the main part of the house. He knocked once on the ceiling but Rolando didn't answer, he tried the knock again, yet he didn't get a response from below. Concerned about the silence he grabbed his 9mm and made his way out of the house through a roof vent that led to a drop ceiling on to the back of the home. He quietly peeked through the kitchen window, thinking that perhaps something was wrong, but the house was empty, as was the barn where the Bug was kept.

Bewildered by the circumstances, Pablo decided to hide underneath the wooden frame home where he could see the highway and anyone driving up to the house.

Soon after the night had fallen upon the countryside, the resident critters surfaced ubiquitously around him. Just as he was ready to leave and go back to the attic hideaway, Pablo noticed headlights approaching in the distance. Unable to see who it was, he prepared for the worst. As the car approached in the darkness of the night, Pablo soon realized that it was Rolando, but he wasn't alone. By the time the Volkswagen Bug had come to a complete stop, like a ghost, Pablo made his way around the barn and to the back of the

Volkswagen. This was a volatile situation with little room for error.

As soon as the unknown passenger opened the door, Pablo placed his gun on the back of his hood covered head and whispered. "Get out of the car slowly."

Rolando seeing what was taking place tried to calm Pablo down signaling with his open palms that everything was okay. The hooded passenger slowly made his way out of the car, and then with a sudden thrust, Pablo threw him on the ground, placing a knee on the back of his head. Pablo then heard a lamenting feminine voice coming from underneath the hood.

"Stop—you are hurting me!" she said!

Pablo immediately stood up looking startled, yet holding his weapon in attack mode while pointing it straight at the mystery person's head.

"Who is it Rolando? I am not in the mood for games." Rolando looked back at Pablo with a disgusted look on his face, and then proceeded to assist his friend to her feet. He then pulled the hood off, and Olga's beautiful dirt-filled face was revealed as she coughed and wiped herself from the mess Pablo had made of her.

Rolando immediately went for his pad to explain the situation, but Pablo stopped him.

"No not now Rolando," he exclaimed feeling breathless from the shock of seeing Olga again. "Let us go inside, it's not safe out here."

Pablo apologized to Olga who smiled with a sparkle in her large brown eyes revealing her forgiveness. The three made their way inside the home where Rolando wrote on his pad while Pablo and Olga stared at each other paralyzed in the moment—not knowing what to say.

"Listen," wrote Rolando, "earlier today I invited Olga to visit my home; I didn't say anything to her about you until we were on our way here. I apologize but I thought you would be pleased."

Pablo didn't' respond, he scratched his head and walked away not knowing what to say. On the one hand, he was glad to see her but on the other hand, he also knew how dangerous it was to have her know about him, especially knowing she was a Communist Party Member.

Olga couldn't help herself from speaking. She lifted her eyes toward Pablo and said, "Pablo, I am sorry if we caused you any grief, but I insisted on coming here. I never thought I'd get to see you again and when Rolando told me about you..." she then began to cry.

Appreciative yet cautious, Pablo walked towards her and the two embraced. Rolando prudently walked away realizing his emotions had overtaken him. Pablo then pulled away.

"I am sorry Olga, but I am married and so are you?"

"Yes," she immediately responded, "but only legally"

"What do you mean?" Pablo asked interested.

"It means that I have never loved my husband. My father made me marry him for political reasons. Jorge is a high ranking government official and my father thought he would take care of me and our family. But what my father didn't know is that my husband is abusive."

"I am sorry Olga—I didn't mean to upset you."

"It's okay," she said wiping the tears from her face.

Meanwhile Rolando stood nearby feeling Olga's pain as his own. He then excused himself and walked out of the house to allow them privacy. Pablo and Olga chatted for a while, but that was as far as it would go. Pablo knew he loved his wife and although Olga would have loved to be with him, Pablo was loyal to a fault. He walked Olga to the car and once again they embraced before she walked away without looking back at the man who she truly loved. Pablo remained touched by the experience, but he was irrefutably committed to the job at hand.

Rolando pulled the Bug around. Olga quickly jumped inside and they drove away. In the house, Pablo drank his coffee slowly as the Bug faded in the distant glare of the rising sun. Too much had happened in too little time and he couldn't avoid the emotions of seeing his childhood sweetheart again. No young person should have so much to think about, he thought. Then he thought of his old patriot friend Demetrio, who often reminded him that he would suffer much for caring much.

He figured that's the way God wanted it to be. He had always hoped to see Olga again; perhaps Rolando knew that seeing her again would cleanse him of his lingering burden, so he could have a clear mind when the moment came to take the shot. Upon his return, Rolando found Pablo sitting silently in a dark corner of the room with the gun strategically resting on his lap. Noticing Pablo's posture, Rolando immediately knew something was wrong. Rolando sat slowly with eyes firmly fixed upon his old friend. Pablo sat motionless not making eye contact—he stared through the window into the open space in obvious discontent.

"Why did you do it—why did you bring her here?" He calmly asked.

Rolando shook his head bewildered by Pablo's radical change in attitude. He raised his hands, shrugging his shoulders as if to ask Pablo what he meant.

"Why did you bring her here? She is married to a government official and if pressed, she might talk."

Concerned, Rolando reached into his back pocket for his writing pad, Pablo raised his weapon, this time pointing it at Rolando's head. Rolando raised his hand in the air then motioned his intent to reach for his pad. He then proceeded to write down his answer.

"Is that why you're upset?" Rolando wrote with a smirk on his face. Not getting a response from Pablo, Rolando continued.

"I didn't mean any harm—I just felt it would be good for you to reconnect with your past. Besides you didn't seem upset an hour ago! He wrote sarcastically and threw the pad at Pablo upset, then walked off into the kitchen. Pablo realizing Rolando's wholesome intention followed him to the kitchen knowing he was genuinely upset.

"Listen Rolando, I didn't mean to upset you," Pablo said apologetically. "It's just that I…, I have been zeroed in on this mission for a long time and as you and I know a lot of people are depending on us to succeed. The last thing I need is to get soft with a woman."

Rolando picked-up his pad. "On the contrary, a man needs the love of a woman to fight for what he believes in," he wrote with passion in his eyes.

"I have a wife Rolando, and besides, what do you know about a woman's love? You were always scared of girls when we were young!" Pablo responded with a slow smile breaking across his face.

"Oh, when a minute ago you wanted to kill me, now you are cracking on me, huh? You know what you need?" Rolando wrote upset. "You need a shrink! That's what you need," he wrote pointing his finger to his own head then walked away again.

"Alright, alright, I am sorry!" Pablo replied raising his voice while following him.

Without turning, Rolando stopped briefly as to acknowledge the apology, and then continued walking towards the back of the house. As he turned the doorknob to open it, an overpowering force from the other side, pushed the door slamming him to the wall behind causing him to fall. Before Rolando could regain his composure, the masked man dressed in army fatigues rushed inside with weapon in hand and placed his boot on Rolando's throat while swinging his gun around in the direction of the kitchen where the two had been before.

"Where is your guest, you damn mute?"

Rolando didn't respond he just shook his head as if to say he didn't know. Without hesitation the man reached to his side pulling a plastic strap from his pants. He flipped Rolando on his stomach, hard-pressing his face down on the floor and hog tied his hands to his feet. The stranger then moved cautiously through the house looking behind every corner with weapon raised. He moved guardedly through every room of the old house knowing that his focal target could be in the premises. He searched the old house for a while. Unable to find Pablo he returned to Rolando pushing his face to the floor once again.

"Tell me where he is hiding or I will end your miserable existence."

Rolando didn't respond. From the side of his eye he could see a shadow in the background, so he remained still. The assailant became furious at Rolando's silence. Just as he prepared to hit him with the gun, the intruder heard a voice from the rear as the cold feel of metal pressed on his neck paralyzing him.

"Drop it and get on your knees or I will splatter your brains all over this room," Pablo said while pressing the point of his 9mm harder on the back of his head. The stunned stranger then dropped his gun without resistance and lifted his arms. Pablo then tied the assailant's hands behind his back and slammed him to the wall. Pablo pulled his hunting knife out from his boot and cut the strap ties from Rolando's hands and legs. Having been humiliated and angry, Rolando stood up and cold cocked the masked intruder knocking him out, and then tied him up.

Pablo calmly stood by silently celebrating his friend's display of anger. They knew the government's way of doing business with the enemy—*move in, kill, ask question later*. This was Castro's way of taking care of castoffs in society. The question remained, who was the motionless person on the floor? Moving quickly Rolando removed the prowler's hooded mask off his head revealing his shocking identity—it was Raton!

Knowing of the potential danger, Pablo proceeded to walk outside and into the darkness of the moonless night with weapon firmly held by his side. After carefully combing the surrounding area of the farm, Pablo returned to the house convinced of the absence of additional accomplices. Visibly angered he walked into the house and in the direction where Raton laid unconscious. Pouring a glass of water on his face, Pablo screamed.

"Despierta carbon" "Wake up you bastard." Pablo yelled out while Rolando nudge his head lightly with his shoe. Raton slowly began to open his eyes, baffled by his unexpected predicament he pretended to be confused.

"Que pasó? What happened?"

Irritated, Rolando cocked his right arm back once again ready to unload yet another numbing blow to Raton's face thinking he had turned on them.

"*Espera,*"or "Wait!" It's not what you think." Raton pleaded.

"You have some explaining to do Sir!" Pablo roared with his body language revealing the dark temper he was known for.

"Allow me to explain, but first loosen these damn straps, they are hurting me"

Pablo nodded for Rolando to let him loose while the cylinder of his silencer now pointed at Raton's groin.

"Point that stupid gun somewhere else man." Raton exclaimed frustrated while rubbing his jaw and looking at Rolando in disgust.

"Listen! If anyone ought to be upset is me! I called you last night and neither of you answered the phone. Where in hell were you? You both knew to wait for the call *coño* or damn it. I thought you had sold-out! Where were you, why didn't you answer the phone?" Raton persisted. Pablo and

Rolando looked at each other briefly realizing that Raton had a point.

"What do you mean?" Pablo asked with an attitude of discontent, yet knowing that Raton had a reason to be upset.

"You know what I mean! From now on, we do not miss an assignment—*Me'entienden?*"

Pablo and Rolando remained suspiciously silent.

"Why did you call?" Pablo asked.

"In line with our agreement, I was to call when the Bastard was on the move—remember? Well, the Bastard is on the move and we have to head out immediately." Raton responded boldly, then turned and walked away.

Chapter Eleven

Insomnia

For a moment there, they had wondered about Raton's authenticity in the plot, but no longer was that the case. Raton was for real and he was determined to fulfill his part of the bargain of seeing the attack through. Realizing the time to move had arrived, Pablo and Rolando went for their belongings. Within minutes the three were on Highway 12 once again, this time traveling back east towards the Trinidad Mountains where the rest of the team waited.

The closer they got to their destination, the more surreal it all appeared. Military activity had intensified on the old country road leading to Trinidad. This was additional proof that Raton's knowledge of the Bastard's whereabouts was accurate. Concerned with the military mobilization, Raton asked Pablo to put on his fuzzy beard disguise and Cuban baseball cap.

"If they stop us, you lie down and act drunk, we are taking you home, *M'entiendes?*"

"Yes sir."

Traveling at high speeds and with headlights turned off, guided only by the soft moonlight, Raton had made it to Trinidad before the sun had proclaimed its place on the far horizon. Once off the main road, Raton drove deep into the rough mountainside terrain and on to the *Bohio* or farmers hut, belonging to one of Raton's accomplices. Upon arrival Raton strategically drove his pickup under the *platanar* or canopy of banana trees on the opposite side of the rural hut. Without hesitation, the three of them walked into the *Bohio* through its rear door.

"Have a seat, I will be right back." Raton whispered, as to not disturb the family members who were asleep on the other side of the home. He then disappeared through a cloth sheet which served as a makeshift door between rooms. The word on the accomplice and his family was that they were part of the plot, but didn't want to be identified.

Looking at Rolando, Pablo knew he wasn't feeling comfortable with the situation. His eyes traveled apprehensively through every inch of the small back room where the two waited under the light of a single candle on the wooden table next to them. On the other side of a sheet separating them from the rest of the shack, voices could be heard—one of them Raton's. After a few minutes he appeared holding a large black bag under his arm. Raton walked in their direction and placed the bag on the table next to the now half burned candle.

"Here is the Bastard's medication boy."

Pablo didn't quite know what to make of it. With new found trust in Raton, he stood and walked towards the bag intently looking into Raton's eyes for any signs of weakness. Standing over the battered old bag, Pablo reached for it cautiously sliding the rusted zipper back far enough to reveal its content. Realizing it was the M21 sniper rifle, he stuck his hand further inside the bag making sure the silencer and ammunition was with it. He then turned his sight toward Rolando whose eyes revealed equal commitment to finish what they had started. In the midst of the tense moment Pablo spoke.

"What now?" he asked.

Raton nodded, winking his left eye with assuring confirmation.

"It's time to go boy," he responded, and without hesitation walked out of the home and towards the truck. Pablo picked up the bag from the table and also walked out followed closely by Rolando.

The journey had been exhausting in every way. Unable to control the voices in his brain, Pablo had not slept well in three weeks. Exhausted from the insomnia caused by contradicting thoughts of killing another man, Pablo's mind had become a hostage of his own conscience. Even so, he moved ahead with the planned attack, motivated only by his lifelong hatred of the man he despised most in life.

"Rolando, tell me you will contact my family if I don't make it out alive." Pablo requested as the two walked towards the truck. Rolando nodded as if to say, *don't worry, I will.*

Morning was now approaching and the roosters were up early making their proclamation of the coming sun.

"Some things never change, do them Rolando? I don't know about you, but I can't get enough of roosters. Did you know that I never heard a rooster crow in Milwaukee?"

Rolando shrugged his shoulders as if to say, who gives a damn!

Upon reaching the truck Pablo sat in the front passenger seat while Rolando kept watch outside for Raton. Pablo took the rifle out of the bag and checked it to make sure of its functionality. He placed the silencer on and loaded one round of ammunition; he then shot into the *platanar*, splitting a number of trees in half.

Raton arrived soon after, quickly driving out of the farm and onto the mountainside dirt road which would eventually lead them to the tactical location selected for Pablo's attack.

"The table is set for you boy." Raton said confidently while driving. "We have word confirming the Bastard is on his way."

Pablo didn't respond, he just looked at Raton with tired eyes, and then looked straight ahead with renewed passion, knowing the time of truth was imminent. One way or another it would soon be over.

As they approached the secret location, Raton pulled over to a lookout point on the east side of the mountain overlooking the distant city of Trinidad and beyond it the Caribbean Sea. Turning off the engine he stepped out of truck and asked Pablo and Rolando to follow him.

"*Vengan*" or "Come-on and bring your scope, let me show you something." he said firmly. Raton was proud of his plan and he knew every dot in the mission had to be connected. Walking to the edge of the mountain, he pointed south in the direction of a tile roof home hardly visible within the hazy mountain dawn of his beloved Cuban morning.

"You see that house in the distance? That's the Bastard's hideaway." Raton said while pointing to a home hidden away underneath an umbrella of Flamboyán, *or* Royal Poinciana trees.

"That is where Dalia Del Valle, the Bastard's girlfriend lives. The two are planning on getting married soon and the bastard visits her frequently."

Pablo looked through his riffle scope towards the well kept compound, bordered by a concrete fence with cut glass on top for additional protection. Carefully scrutinizing its surroundings, Pablo took his time looking around the grounds of the home. Noticing a wide space between the house and the side of the mountain, Pablo paused. Could this be an escape route he wondered? Pablo took his eye off the scope and looked at Raton as he began to ask…

"I know what you see boy," Raton said before Pablo had a chance to speak. "It has all been figured out—don't worry. If you look on the northwest side of the home and on the other side of that wide space, you will see the road which leads to the front gate. There is always two security guards on duty, one at the front gate and the other walks around the home every five minutes or so. These are well trained Special Forces guards who we need to eliminate as soon as possible after the Bastard is down. When you shoot the Bastard, shoot that guard next, he is a local and knows the area well. If you don't kill them—they will kill you!

Pablo's attention intensified with every word Raton spoke. "To the right of the front gate is the house where the dogs are kept. These are the security guards dogs and they only listen to him. You kill their master; the dogs will not chase you after the attack. More than likely you will have a two second window of time to take your shot just inside the security wall and the side of the house as the Bastard exits the vehicle and goes to enter the home through its side door. Keep in mind, that although he never enters the home from the front, you have to be prepared for anything," Raton continued to provide Pablo with information in a calm confidant voice.

"According to intelligence, his bodyguard rides in the front seat, his secretary rides with him in the rear. There are always two military jeeps that ride along with the armored vehicle carrying the Bastard, they are Special Forces armed to their teeth. Sometimes they have lookalikes riding with the caravan, but don't be fooled, there is only one Bastard and he never exposes himself for long. Also know that the armored vehicle in which he rides changes frequently, so be alert so as to know the difference,

M'entiendes?" Pablo nodded his head briefly then motioned

with his finger for Raton to continue.

"The front vehicle in the caravan will always stop

approximately twenty feet outside of the gate. The

bodyguard on the driver's side will exit the vehicle to talk to

the security guard at the front gate of the home. After a brief

conversation, he scouted the immediate area on foot. This

usually takes a few minutes as he inspects the fence around

the home and the trees, then he will slowly scan the

surrounding mountain areas with his binoculars. This is

when you must be the most alert; somehow you will need to

hide long enough to not be seen by the guard, yet not so long

as to miss your small window of time for the shot. You must

cancel every thought—ignore every sound around you and

zero in on the target. Sometimes the Bastard likes to go out

of his vehicle before it enters the gate. We don't know why

he does that but whatever the reason, be ready. Once you

have made the decision to go for the shot, you'll have enough time to hit him with a second shot. Shoot the head first, this way if you can't hit him with a second shot and he doesn't die, he will be damaged goods, pissing on himself for the rest of his miserable days on this earth. If you have a clearing after the first shot, expect him to drop and then you'll hit him again on the ground. This time you aim for the heart, *M'entiendes?*" Pablo nodded in affirmation.

"You will then shoot whoever comes to the Bastard's aid, this way you will minimize the chase so we can get away. Keep in mind your effective range is within 900 meters and you have five rounds to do your job. Once you have taken all your shots, you will drop the rifle in the hole, jump out and run like hell down the other side of the mountain— I'll be in my truck waiting for you. *M'entiendes?"*

Silence reigned for a moment as a multitude of thoughts raced through Pablo's mind as he remembered Ramón and Manolo's words about the Salmon. Pablo then stood tall as to proclaim his presence to the wind peacefully looking at his final destination, knowing of the unavoidable conclusion to his journey—kill or be killed. He then bowed his head and prayed.

"Am I really the Salmon, Lord? Is that what I am? If it is not your will for me to be here, please remove me from this place."

Like a hazy dream, Pablo remained silent as if to wait for God's response, knowing that killing another man was not acceptable with the Lord. Not receiving a clear answer, Pablo lifted his head up to the sky and asked for forgiveness knowing forgiveness would not be guaranteed.

Not wanting to interrupt Pablo's thoughts, Raton walked down the mountain a few yards then stopped until Pablo looked at him.

"Get your belongings son, it's time to go."

Pablo went to the truck grabbed his back pack and rifle bag and walked towards Rolando. Without saying a word they hugged holding on to each other for a moment.

"It was good seeing you again my friend." Pablo said with emotion in his voice.

"If I don't make it out alive, please tell my wife, Mama and Esther I loved them." Rolando remained still with his head lowered. He then pulled out his pad and pen and wrote, "I will tell them! But listen Pablo; I can stay here with you, if you'd like."

Pablo shook his head and paused for a moment. "No, this is personal hermano *or* brother, besides, if you don't make out it either, who is going to send my message to my family?" Pablo said with a grin on his face. He then turned and walked away towards Raton. Rolando remained in his place for a moment hoping Pablo would change his mind, but Pablo didn't flinch, he walked away with the conviction of a man on a mission. In his heart, Rolando knew this was

Pablo's fight, so he turned away and walked down the mountain towards the farmer's home where he would remain for a while as agreed upon.

🐟 🐟 🐟

Walking up the mountain Raton showed Pablo the escape route he was to take after the shooting. He then proceeded to take him to the strategic place he had selected for the attempt. Once at the location, Pablo noticed the rough mountain terrain in the immediate area. The dense undergrowth of entangling thorn bushes made it difficult to reach the burrow Raton had carved into the ground.

"Well boy, this is it!" Raton exclaimed.

"This is where what is?" Pablo asked.

Raton giggled briefly with a strong sense of satisfaction.

"This is your residence for the next three days," Raton humorously said. "This is where you will deliver the Bastard's medicine."

Pablo scratched his head thinking Raton was joking.

"Say that again?" Pablo asked wondering what in hell Raton was referring to.

Raton smiled without responding and proceeded to reveal the hideout hole he had concealed underneath thorn bushes.

"Crazy!" Pablo thought. There is no way I am going to spend three days in there. It isn't big enough for a raccoon he thought. He then realized why his new acquaintance had been nicked-named *The Mouse* in prison!

The targeted home below was hard to see from the mountainside location, yet once Pablo crawled into the hole, he appreciated Raton's genius. He had skillfully carved a hole in the ground and trimmed the thorn bushes to such perfection, not even birds would know of Pablo's presence there. The view to Dalia's home was clearly visible, yet impossible to see from below.

"Here it is boy," said Raton while handing Pablo a plastic bag and two gallons, one full of water, the other one empty.

"What's this?" asked Pablo wondering about the content in the bag, as well as the reason for the empty gallon.

"The bag contains six vacuum-packed military meals—you will eat two a day, one in the morning and one in the late afternoon. If the Bastard doesn't show in three days, I am pulling you out, *M'entiendes?*"

"Yes sir! What about the empty bottle?"

"You will urinate in it. Once you fill it, dig a hole in a downhill angle and slowly pour the urine in it then you cover it with dirt. Do not throw it out; the dogs will smell it a mile away.

Also remember to keep enough urine in the bottle in case you run out of water, this way you will have something to drink and not dehydrate. Take out the food packs and use the plastic bag for defecating. In the past, when the Bastard has visited Dalia, sometimes the military brings hound dogs with them; you don't want them to sniff you out. If for some reason they come near the hole, remain cool, dogs don't like thorn bushes. They will bark but not approach you."

With that, Raton shook Pablo's hand, wished him well and walked away only to stop a few feet away and say, "You are a lucky man Pablo—many have tried to silence the voice of the Bastard without success. I used to dream of being the lucky one to take the shot. Planning this moment kept me from going crazy in the torture chambers when I was in prison. In my dreams I could see it all clearly but never did I take the shot—I always woke up too soon."

"Like David, you have been destined to take down the Goliath of today. Think of it this way, Communism is an atheist philosophy. Like Goliath, Castro has defied God. David had five stones, one for Goliath and one for each of the other giant family members. David killed the giant with one stone; you will kill the bastard with one bullet and use the four other rounds for the guards. So be ready, the Bastard

is on his way! *M'entiendes!* Raton then turned and walked

away not looking back again.

Pablo didn't respond, he remained thoughtful,

realizing the magnitude of what was about to take place. He

knew many had died trying to assassinate Fidel in the past.

Raton's words about the biblical account in *1ˢᵗ Samuel 17*

revealed his knowledge of the Word. Upon hearing the

confidence in Raton's words, Pablo was encouraged, yet the

thought of his own death was sobering. Pablo didn't know

much about the Bible other than what Billy had told him

about receiving salvation through the blood of Christ,

repentance and asking Him to come into his heart. But he

knew the story of David and Goliath well. Being small in

stature, David's bravery had encouraged him ever since he

heard the story in the Jesuit Church on San Carlos Street in

Glorytown.

Pablo proceeded to enter the well carved hideaway and settle in the five foot deep by five feet wide hole with great caution. There was enough space for Pablo to sit and stand, but not much more than that.

Overhead, the entangled vines of thorn bushes canopied precisely over the hole, accessible only by slithering on the ground like a snake. Once inside the lonely space, the humid odor of wet mud and rotted roots was unbearable. Even so, Pablo remained determined to see the mission through.

Looking at the fast moving clouds racing across the full moon sky above, he wondered if this would be his final resting place. In turbulent thoughts produced by sleeplessness, he saw his body consumed by maggots feasting on his decomposing corpse.

He tried to close his eyes and rest, but insomnia had set its deep roots of control over him—he was now its slave, his mind flooded with thoughts of demise.

The first sleepless night passed quietly with no action at Dalia's home below. Only the passing by critters knew of his presence in the mountain. With every passing minute, he was becoming one of them. The way he figured it, thinking like an animal was necessary for survival.

The night is a lonely place in the wild Pablo thought; perhaps if the critters hung around long enough, he could chat with them. But they had no interest in him as long as he was alive.

Concerned about his inability to sleep, Pablo knew the dangers of insomnia; his mother had suffered a nervous breakdown once because of it. This is the one thing he feared most—breaking down was not in the plans. The harder he tried to sleep the harder it became.

The following day nothing changed, other than the arrival of vultures dancing in the wind above. Why were they here? Pablo wondered. Could they smell the coming of death below? The day was hot and humid, yet he remained in his solemn place as agreed upon.

With little water to drink, Pablo's mind repeatedly switched from reality to chaotic thoughts of the exhausting, never-ending struggle between what was right and what was wrong. Cold sweats and hallucinating visions of fear and failure began to overpower his iron will.

The second night he almost slept, but the arrival of large foul rats outside the hole wouldn't let him. Pablo didn't fear dying from a bullet, but he was horrified of rats and their disease filled bites. The third night was as uneventful as the first. Dehydrated, hungry and without sleep, Pablo wondered if the Bastard had outsmarted his team.

After hours of waiting, Pablo dozed off long enough to lose his sense of time and place, only to be startled by the distant sound of approaching engines. It was 2:58 A.M, surely this couldn't be the Bastard he thought, but if it wasn't him, who in

the hell could be out driving in the mountains in the middle of the night? He wondered out loud.

He immediately stood up and snatched his night vision binoculars and placed the sniper rifle next to him. Looking into the distant darkness nothing appeared out of the ordinary, yet the sound of bottomless machinery approaching was irrefutable. Holding his breath in the midst of anxiety and fighting off the cold sweat from his forehead, Pablo remained watchful for the first sight of the possible Bastard's caravan.

Minutes passed with no sight of headlights, then like a slow creeping snail, three military vehicles appeared within the distant fog. As they approached Dalia's home, a jeep sped ahead of the other two vehicles stopping a few feet from the front gate of the home.

Two officers with long weapons quickly stepped out of the military vehicle. One quickly approached the security guard at the front gate; the other went to the back of the vehicle

shining a high power flashlight in the immediate area as well as on to the base of the mountain.

Pablo remained still, calculating the distance between him and the approximate place where the Bastard's vehicle would stop once it entered the gate. This was the armored Land Rover intelligence had forewarned him about. He was told Castro always traveled in the passenger side with two well armed bodyguards behind him.

Pablo reached inside the front right pocket of his jacket, pulling out the bullet Ramon had given him in Key West. Fighting off weakness from dehydrating cold sweats, Pablo prepared himself for his long waited moment to slaughter the giant. He loaded the rifle and pointed it in the direction of the home below and waited for the Rover to approach.

After a few minutes, the Rover moved forward slowly, once given the go ahead sign by the guards in front of the home. The gates opened and the Rover quickly slipped inside of Dalia's well secured compound. Perspiring profusely and struggling to see clearly through the hazy fog, Pablo remained poised, taking aim, ready to pull the trigger at any second. Knowing now the window of time and space was minimized as one of the guards standing outside the Rover capriciously approached the driver of the main vehicle while talking on the radio. Unaware of what was taking place; Pablo quickly transferred his rifle sight to the passenger door of the Rover once again. He wondered if this was an intelligence move to slip the Bastard into the house through the other side of the vehicle.

The conversation between the two guards lasted only seconds, but in Pablo's anxious mind it seemed an eternity. The moment of truth was upon him, the question was, could he pull the trigger? What if he didn't, what would he tell Raton, Manolo and Ramón? Would he then become the target instead of the Bastard? A million thoughts went through his mind in the split second that it took for the Bastard to step out of the Rover and begin to walk into the house.

Then it happened, the large figure of the man he hated slowly stepped out of the vehicle. He stretched a bit and then as if he knew of Pablo's presence in the mountain, the Bastard defiantly looked directly at him. There is no way he could have known Pablo's whereabouts; this is not how it is supposed to be, Pablo whispered to himself. Even the sheep are blindfolded when slaughtered, he thought.

"Look the other way you fool," he said infuriated. "I am the Salmon and I am finishing my run, you bastard!"

Just as he was about to pull the trigger, Pablo remembered his grandparents' words once again, "If you execute your plan, you are no less a murderer that Castro is."

Consumed by the guilt of disappointing his grandparents, Pablo paused to stretch-out his cramping right hand. He hit it against the ground to create blood flow, never taking his eyes off the target through the rifle scope, knowing the opening for the shot would be brief. His stress intensified and his vision became blurred by the relentless perspiration dripping from his forehead.

He wiped his face once on the sleeve of his shirt then quickly flattened his eye socked against the scope of the rifle. Pablo wanted the first shot to count, so he zeroed in on the bastard's right temple. He took a deep breath and holding it long enough to hear his heart denounce the murder he was about to commit, Pablo pulled the trigger unloading the five round. In a sobering moment of profound regret for having executed the plot to kill another man, Pablo immediately looked to the sky as if to ask for forgiveness. He then dropped the riffle and crawled out of the musty hole in the ground and ran. Weakened from dehydrating fatigue and with legs like concrete pillars, Pablo couldn't move, he fell to the ground. He had refused to drink his own urine when he ran out of water, now he was being paralyzed by crippling spasms which condemned his broken spirit with fear and shame. Unable to stand again, Pablo laid on the ground facing the sky, begging for mercy from above. He tried to stand time and time again, but his legs did not respond. He then heard the sound of dogs approaching.

The wind became stronger as the clouds clashed in the angry skies above, while glowing lightening crashed the earth, setting trees on fire. "Hell! This is hell," Pablo screamed repentantly within the furnace his world had become. Just as he was about to be consumed by the fire…he sat up tormented and drenched in persperation from the horrifying struggle. With eyes wide open Pablo looked around the room not knowing where he was. It was the middle of the night and after weeks of restless nights he had finally collapsed and fallen into a deep sleep on the living room floor.

"Please hide, the rats are coming—hurry up, hide!" he screamed with terror in his voice. Realizing it had been a hallucinating nightmare and bewildered by the horror he had just experienced, he stood up and looked around hoping to recognize the surroundings. Alone and scared, the eerie silence of the night, revealed Pablo's greatest fear—he was losing his mind.

He remained standing, as if to gather his breathless thoughts, his notion of time had been raddled. After a few minutes of silence, he sat down with his face buried in the clammy palms of his hands, finally realizing he was safe at home. In the raddled depths of his isolation, Pablo went over the dream in his mind, realizing that it had been the execution of the well planned attack on Castro. For too long he had gone over every step of the attack until it became engraved deeply into his subconscious. Wondering if God was trying to tell him something, Pablo then questioned if he could live with the burden of having killed another man. He didn't feel Fidel Castro deserved to live, but who was he to decide. The pressure had been enormous and he knew that if he continued in the path he was going, he would certainly crack.

Pablo then thought of what he once heard in the streets of his hometown when he was young. 'You don't sleep—you go crazy!' Was he losing his mind, or had he already broken down? He wondered. Perhaps it was part of the personal cleansing process he had been sentenced to endure. Perhaps it was part of the great sacrifice some men had to accept to impact the world in a favorable way. Pablo also wondered why some men are dammed with the burden of seeing justice done. Perhaps he was one of those poor souls who were destined to live in the misery of his flawed ways, unable to live peacefully, as most men do. But then again, he never wanted to be like those who never step outside of their comfort zones for the sake of doing a good deed, even if they have to risk it all.

Seeing his father die young had awakened Pablo to the reality that time on earth is short, and windows of opportunity to do the right thing diminish with every passing day. Pablo understood he wasn't perfect, but he didn't want to be like those who live their lives in obscurity, happy to exist in their perceived sense of security. Moving through the day-to-day revolving door of life until it ends—so he patiently waited. .

Chapter Twelve

Freedom Found

From a distance, Pablo observed as the Mariel Harbor exodus in Habana had become the focal point of the world. Human rights organizations from across the globe were by then putting pressure on the United Nations to act once and for all. Seeing the world-wide support to get the dissidents safely out of Cuba; Fidel remained at his post in Habana, to make sure everyone who wanted to leave Cuba would do so. He knew many of them represented a great oppositional threat if they were to remain in the island. As a result, over one hundred thousand men; women and children left Cuba and on to freedom in America through what became known as the historic Mariel Harbor exodus.

Conceivably, this was divine intervention after all. With the waters between Cuba and America full of refugees going north and U.S. Coast Guard vessels overseeing the exodus, a fishing boat with two Cuban-Americans going south would no longer have been so innocuous-looking. Nobody would believe they were going fishing or had gotten lost—they didn't have a prayer of landing in Cuba unnoticed.

In addition to the Mariel Harbor madness, news from Miami regarding two unknown men having been captured by Castro forces as they attempted to infiltrate the island was not encouraging. Their objective was unclear, but the word in the streets was that the two were also on a mission to get to Fidel and that Castro forces were waiting for them on the shorelines. Like sitting ducks, they were caught, paraded through the town as propaganda, and then executed by a firing squad within twenty four hours. To Pablo, this was clear evidence that Castro spies were among their exile group.

Pablo was passionate for freedom, but he wasn't a fool—he knew the regime had its tentacles in America. As confirmation of his intuition, later that week he received word from Punson, 'the plan is delayed' Punson officially announced in a coded message. "Stand by for further instructions." Pablo was relieved to hear the message, but he also knew that Ramón must have been furious and it wouldn't be long before we engaged in another plot to kill the Baststard.

In the days to follow, life went back to normal, the folks continued to meet at the park, the group waited for word from Miami. As if nothing had happened, Pablo remained in leadership at the park rallies, heading over youth involvement and recruitment. The group conducted press releases and a massive food drive which collected over one hundred thousand pounds of canned food and other items to send to Peru. This is where many of the earlier occupants of the Embassy in Habana had been sent for protection from Cuban authorities. From what was reported, their living conditions there weren't very favorable. To Pablo, the fact that the most courageous young men involved in storming the Peruvian Embassy had to suffer such consequences in Peru was inconceivable.

The team involved in the plot waited for news from Ramón for days, but news never reached them. Although somewhat disappointed, Pablo knew the timing was bad. Nonetheless, he was happy that so many more Cuban people, whom had suffered under the Castro regime, would be finding their freedom in America, as he and his family had found their own. He just hoped that through the living testimony of ten thousand Embassy crashers desperate to leave the island prison of Cuba, the world would understand how bad the Castro regime really was. Fortunately, the media jumped on the story early on, but unfortunately news revealing the truth about why the people risked it all to be free was never clearly stated.

Suspecting the mission had ended before it had begun; Pablo slowly began to accept the possibility that he

would never get to realize his dream of freeing the Cuban
people. He struggled greatly with feelings of disappointment
knowing there was unfinished business. Pablo had prepared
himself well for the challenge, but it had all been in vain.

The months that followed were very dark for him.
For weeks, he had psyched himself up in preparation for a
clandestine insertion into hostile territory. He had imagined
a thousand times what it would be like to kill another human
being—not just Castro, but possibly his guards, the police,
or military personnel as well. It had even occurred to him
that if some Castro-sympathizing civilian had caught wind
of what the group was plotting, they would have to eliminate
them as well. That was not something he was looking
forward to, but the more hardened members of the operation
would get it done, for the sake of carrying out the attack. In
Pablo's heart he knew that he wasn't a cold hearted killer
like Ramón, but he felt this was a

noble cause and personal feelings paled in comparison to the ultimate goal.

Frustrated, Pablo knew he had to redirect his anger. Like a time bomb, he walked around bitter and angry— nothing appeared to make any sense. The summer passed uneventfully, then fall came and the Mariel Harbor boatlifts ceased in late October. Perhaps that would be a good time to revisit the plan, but by then Pablo had lost his connections as well as his interest in preparing for another attempt. He had grown detached and unwell, as the resentment of losing his Papa intensified. Life as he knew it had radically changed and redirecting it for the good of those he loved, would be difficult and he knew it.

Nineteen Eighty passed by quickly, as did Nineteen Eighty-One, yet the thought of living a normal life scared him. Up to that point, life had battered him since childhood, being a normal person didn't fit him. In his darkest moments, the thought of his Abuela's words appeased him.

"Don't become like them," she had told him years before. "If you let your heart be filled with hate, then you will be no better than the Communists." She would often remind him."

In the depths of his heart, Pablo was afraid that loved ones would be very disappointed in him if they knew of his involvement with a plot to kill. The hate inside him had spilled over long ago, and he had committed murder so often in his heart that he was practically a serial killer, according to his Abuela's way of seeing things. Pablo didn't necessarily think that imagining murder was the same as committing it, but none the less, it was wrong and he knew it.

In the midst of his emotional storm, Pablo was certain of one thing, his Abuelo's were happy that he and his family had escaped the Castro's iron grip on them and they had made it to freedom in America. And so, little by little, Pablo began to wake up to the fact that if he didn't make anything of himself, it wasn't America's fault—it was my own.

In America, where freedom was sometimes taken for granted, Pablo could do anything, become anything, dream of anything, and not be persecuted for it. The more he thought about it, the more he began to come around.

What was he doing, pretending to be a hit man? Although Pablo knew he could have carried out the attempt successfully, he also knew it was wrong before God's eyes. What he needed to do was get his focus back and do the right thing for his family. Little by little, he had to stop being so angry, it was ruining his life, and he had to get it under control before it ruined his relationships with loved ones. The thought of a family of his own was prevalent in his mind. Did he want to be a thug, or did he want to be the kind of father his Papa had been—patient, loving and kind, despite endless hardships?

There was only one right answer to that question, and deep inside his heart Pablo knew it. The gap between where he was and where he wanted to be was insurmountably huge, he felt. How could he just stop being himself? Pablo needed help.

There are no quick fixes in life, he thought. This was a lesson he had learned throughout his young life. Although he would not transform overnight, he could begin working on himself little by little. Putting hatred aside was the key, the question was—could he do it?

Pablo decided that God had a greater purpose for his life in taking the assassination attempt out of his path. Although he didn't fear dying for a just cause, Pablo didn't want to die just yet. He wanted to live long enough to have a family, and to enjoy his children and his grandchildren in his golden years. He also wanted to pass on to them what had been passed down to him, a legacy of integrity as a foundation for their lives.

The more he separated himself from those involved in the planning of the attack, the clearer his perspective became. Pablo wanted to work hard to leave the next generation equipped with a business, or some property, or anything they could use as a starting point in their own lives. They would know about his pursue of freedom for the Cuban people, but most importantly, they would know how to treasure and defend their own freedom in America.

To know that his children would be a few steps ahead of where he was when he started out in America mattered to him. This was the only right way to live. Would he really be helping the world by killing Fidel? Perhaps, but what would become of himself Pablo thought? Could he live with himself even if he succeeded and survived the attempt? These were the type of questions which kept him up at nigh now—questions worth losing sleep over.

Slowly, Pablo came to understand something: Fidel himself, despite his great personal culpability, was not the only problem. The real problem was Communism. It preyed on the ignorant and the poor by making promises of a better tomorrow, yet delivering deceit. *Don't worry, government will provide the people everything,* they say, while killing the freedom spirit of self-sufficiency and personal responsibility, with the ultimate objective of dummying down people so they depend on government to think for themselves.

At his young age, Pablo had already seen the true face of the Socialist Communist. The government disguises itself as a virtuous and fervent defender of the poor, while funneling wealth and resources to its elite party members.

Life had changed for Pablo. To understand the sacrifice made by his parents was to understand his responsibility of doing the right thing in contributing to elevate his adopted motherland—the United States of America. Every time he achieved something in life, whether it was something simple, like having a successful business, worshiping God freely, or something major, like publishing a book—it was another slap in the face to his totalitarian regime. The Commander and Chief and his lieutenants had tried to crush his spirit under their heels, being considered to be nothing but a worm, but they had failed! And so it was that Pablo began to put a new life together for himself.

In 1979, God had sent a messenger to rescue Pablo, he's name was Billy. Almost twenty years later in 1996, God used a different type of servant to rescue him—a Godly man by the name of John. Senator, John Grant had been involved in the leadership of the 1979 Billy Graham crusade. Having seen Pablo interviewed on television regarding other community matters, Mr. Grant called Pablo and asked if he would be interested in participating in an organizational committee to bring Billy Graham back to Tampa for an evangelical crusade.

Dumbfounded by the call, Pablo began to see Gods purpose for his life and he happily accepted the Senators invitation. For the following two years, the organizational committee worked fervently on the enormous task of raising the two million dollar budged forth crusade, as well as the recruitment of church leaders, logistics and other key matters.

In the blink of an eye, the 1998 Tampa Bay Crusade Billy Graham Crusade became the first non football event at the Tampa, Raymond James Stadium. In a few short years, life had taken Pablo for a whirlwind of a ride. From once having been an active member in the planning of an assassination attempt—to the leadership committee to help organize the Tampa Bay Billy Graham Crusade. This was the same man who had once led him to accept Christ as he's Lord and savior. This wasn't a coincidence, and Pablo knew it God had a purpose for his life. When darkness had once overtaken his existence, God had other plans for him. Little did he know what lied ahead—perhaps no one ever knows!

🐟 🐟 🐟

Once the opening day of the four day crusade came and the doors of the newly constructed Tampa stadium opened, Pablo was amazed by the large turnout and diversity of the people who couldn't wait to go inside of the stadium. Like ants, they quickly took over the grounds, as well as the 65,000 seats. Over the next few days Pablo remained in awe of the momentous experience.

Never could he have imagined such an awesome manifestation of kindness and love displayed by the orderly crowds. Young and old, black and white, tattooed bikers with long hair and dirty looking beards, mingled with one another in a sea of excitement, rejoicing in the moment. That wasn't supposed to be—but it was! Folks didn't see the color of each other's skin, nor could they tell the difference between teased hair and nose rings. They were all one in spirit, anxiously waiting to hear Billy's encouraging message about the unconditional love of God.

On Sunday the 25th of October, 1998 knowing it was the last day of the crusade and the end of a wonderful two year journey. Pablo spent a significant amount of time walking around and absorbing the moment, knowing that he may never have a chance to see Billy Graham in person again. Billy then stepped-up to the microphone and like the three previous nights, people applauded and chanted Billy, Billy, Billy…

Pablo then sat back surrounded by his family and listened carefully to every word Billy expressed, knowing the significance of the moment. Billy shared his normal greeting with the audience and then began to preach his message of forgiveness from the book of Jonah.

Billy started his message by saying, "God gave a Jonah a second chance after he had ran away hoping to avoid going to Nineveh, a place of imposing military might and the place where Israel's enemy resided. Nineveh was the heart and the center of the nation of Assyria, a sleeping giant that would eventually look to annihilate Israel. Jonah wanted no part of going there."

He paused for a second and looking up he asked, "Is God calling you to serve?" Jesus came to serve not to be served." Billy reminded all who listened attentively, without hesitation; he lowered his head and read from the word of God.

"The Lord commanded Jonah to tell the wicked people of Nineveh, a city north of Babylon, that if they didn't repent, they would be destroyed. Jonah didn't want to go to that wicked place. He didn't think the people would listen to him or want to change, so he got on a boat that was sailing west to Tarshish, Spain, hoping to avoid the presence of God. A terrifying storm arose and tossed the boat to and fro. The sailors cried out to the prophet who was sleeping, to please pray to his God to save them. Knowing that his disobedience was the cause of the storm, Jonah told them,

"Take me up, and cast me forth into the sea; so shall the sea be calm unto you" (Jonah 1:12)

"Though they didn't want to, the sailors finally did as Jonah asked and threw him into the sea. Now the Lord had prepared a great fish to swallow up Jonah. And Jonah was in the belly of the fish three days and three nights." (Jonah 1:17).

While in the fish, Jonah cried unto the Lord. He knew that he had disobeyed, and he wanted the Lord to forgive him. The Lord did, then caused the fish to vomit out Jonah upon the dry land" Jonah 2:10. He again told the prophet to go to Nineveh. Jonah obeyed, to Gods surprise. When he told the people of Nineveh that the Lord was displeased with them and that they would soon be destroyed, they believed him and turned from their evil ways. They accepted the gift of repentance that would come through the Savior, and they were not destroyed. Both the prophet and the people he preached to have the need for the atoning sacrifice of Jesus

Christ, so that they could return to the Heavenly Father. Because this gift is given to everyone, we too can repent when we make mistakes. Our God is a loving and forgiving God."

As Billy preached on, the words of poet, Francis Thompson in his poem, The Hound of Heaven slowly reached the heart of Pablo, convicting him for his hatred towards Castro and every single communist who had ever mistreated him and his family. He remembered the essence of the poem, where the hound follows the hare, never ceasing in its running, ever drawing nearer in the chase, with firm conviction and unperturbed pace, so does God follow the fleeing soul by His Divine grace. And though in sin or in human love, away from God it seeks to hide itself, Divine grace unwearyingly follows ever after, till the soul feels its pressure forcing it to turn to Him alone in that never ending pursuit.

Billy preached on. "Jonah didn't want to go to Nineveh because he knew the Ninevites were some of the cruelest people in the history of the world. So he tried to run away from God. He got on a ship and left for another land. A storm came and Jonah ended up in the turbulent sea where a giant fish ate him—spending three days and three nights in the belly of the big fish.

Jonah later repented and went to Nineveh and preached of God's love and the whole city repented; even the king. One of these days you will want to repent of your ways, but it might be too late." Pablo listened knowing of the hatred he had harbored in his heart for forty years, as Billy continued hammering the word.

"After it was over, Jonah remained angry, he didn't want to see the people of Nineveh saved. So he went to a high place on a mountain overlooking the city to see if the people had really changed from their ways. God then provided Jonah a vine and made it grow over him to provide shade from the burning sun. Seeing that Jonah remained angry, God provided a worm which chewed the vine so that it withered, the Bible says. He then provided a scorching east wind and the sun blazed on Jonah's head and he grew faint. Jonah complained to God—he wanted to die. Then God said to Jonah, *'do you have the right to be angry about the vine?'*

"Yes, angry enough to die." Jonah responded. Billy preached with greater fervor.

"But the Lord said *'you are angry about the vine, though you did not grow it. But Nineveh has more than seven hundred thousand people and I am not to be concerned about them?'* God asked Jonah."

Billy then stopped speaking for a moment; Pablo noticed there was an eerie silence in the stadium. Only the yielding sound of folks sobbing of conviction could be heard—Pablo among them. In that moment of reflection he understood the errors of his ways in having hated another man enough to ruthlessly want to end his life. Burdened with guilt, Pablo bowed his head and asked the Lord to forgive him for his hatred. Soon after that moment and under overwhelming sense of conviction, Pablo forgave Fidel Castro for all the pain he had caused him.

Immediately, a feeling peace took over Pablo, as he turned his hatred of Castro over to God.

Inexplicably, that sobering decision helped Pablo realize that the hatred in his heart had allowed the dictator to continue violating his day to day life. In forgiving him, Pablo had liberated himself of the tormenting burden of life draining hate. Once again Billy Graham had been used by God as an instrument of His Glory in Pablo's life. For the first time since the early days of his childhood, Pablo felt spiritually free. As a child he didn't really understand freedom, all he had known was family love and happiness. Then Castro came to power and freedom was taken away when he was five years old. That was when his hatred for one man had begun— allowing vicious anger to dictate much of his life.

Long after the crusade was over and emotionally drained, Pablo rejoiced over his change of heart. He was grateful for the remarkable two year journey of planning the Billy Graham Crusade. This had proven to be his journey to spiritual freedom.

When, for so long, Pablo had yearned to be free in America, he didn't realize that true freedom is not a physical matter, but a spiritual one. Pablo had finally found it in forgiving one man.

Although Pablo had made his choice to follow Jesus long ago, the lingering question for him remained...could he go back to Cuba if God called for him to go and face the regime he blamed for violating his childhood? Like Jonah, Pablo wanted God to Judge Castro and every single Communist, for all the wrong they had done to the Cuban people.

Although he remained strongly opposed to the regime's violations of human rights against the Cuban people, Pablo had chosen to leave the reprisal in God's hands. Difficult as it was, he had to regularly remind himself of what Jesus would do is his place. Pablo regularly had to remind himself of the Christ who asked the Father to forgive those who spit on Him, beat Him and ultimately nailed Him onto a rugged wooden cross till death came upon Him.

"You're the Salmon Boy," the old man said to him in his dreams—Pablo remembered those words all too well. Could this have been a divine message to make him see the wrong of his hatred and his violent ways? Was he really the salmon, or was he a poor fool who had lost his way? Perhaps it was possible that like the salmon, he was destined to someday return to his natal stream and spawn the message of spiritual freedom, rather than to shed another man's blood. Pablo told God on that cool October evening in 1998, that unlike Jonah, he wouldn't run away from doing His will

and so he forgave the one man responsible for his lost childhood.

Billy had originally introduced Pablo to the Lord in 1979, when Graham asked Pablo if he knew where he was going when he died; Pablo didn't know. No one had ever asked him that question before. His whole life, Pablo had been told that his eternal destiny depended on his deeds, church attendance and other complicated matters which contributed to his confusion.

Because of that, he felt that he didn't belong in that eternal home. Why try? As far as he was concerned, it was impossible that a fool like him could ever qualify for heaven.

Overwhelmed with the unattainable task, Pablo had walked away from God. Then as a hound of heaven, Billy reached out in love and brought him back.

"Let me tell you about heaven," he said while revealing the plan of salvation. "You are saved by Grace through faith! There aren't enough good deeds you can do that are good enough to save your own soul." Billy preached. "Man is flawed from Adam and incapable of saving himself through his own works. Good works are the result of your personal relationship with Jesus, and the presence of the Holy Spirit in your heart. Salvation is a gift from God, *for it is by grace you have been saved, through faith—and this is not from yourselves, it is the gift of God—not by works, so that no one can boast.*" (Ephesians 2: 8-9). "Saved by grace through faith, trust and believe in His death and resurrection. It's a gift from God for you and for me," Billy said.

Billy once asked Pablo if he understood the agony Christ had endured for him on the cross to pay for all his sins, so he could have eternal life. Pablo didn't know that type of freedom then and fearful he became. He then knew, and fears he overcame! And now when Pablo dreams...he doesn't dream of rodents or thunderstorms anymore.

Acknowledgments

A special thanks to my wife, Mercy, our sons, Christian, and Gabriel, and their families. My niece, Rebeca, and her family, and special thanks to my grandson Luke— I'm a better person because of you! In memory of two courageous and loving women: my mother, Dionisia, and mother-in-law, Mercedes – I'm eternally grateful for you! Above all, Glory be to God for the Grace that is in Christ Jesus – 2 Timothy 2:1.

Dionisia (Concha) and Mercedes